Get You Out of the Sand

A Common-Sense Approach to Financial Accountability

Lawrence J. Mast

Get Your Head Out of the Sand

Printed in the United States of America
First Printing, 2019
ISBN   978-0-578-50084-3

Robeson House Press
Newport News, VA 23607

Dedication

This book is dedicated to:

My Father, Jacob Mast, who lived a life of good stewardship and effectively used what God gave him. Every missionary who visited our church also visited my dad's garage and walked away with assorted screws, bolts and tools.

My Mother, Donna Mast, who makes every penny count and is the master of the envelope budget.

TABLE OF CONTENTS

Introduction

For over twenty-five years, my wife and I struggled with personal finances. No matter what approach we tried, nothing ever seemed to stop the problem of having no money left at the end of the pay cycle. For over ten years I tracked my finances using various personal finance software programs, but there would be months at a time when I wouldn't even open the software because nothing I did would work.

A friend of mine from church tried to help me get on track with my finances. He loaned me several books that did a good job of explaining how to set up a budget. My situation just didn't quite fit the solutions provided in the book and I had trouble wrapping my head around the concepts presented in the books. I was getting close to a solution but wasn't quite there yet. I was still like an Ostrich with my head in the sand- afraid to check my bank balance or open my mail.

I then heard a business leader explaining the concept of zero-based budgeting in a way that made a lot of sense. I knew that this was what I needed but could not figure out how to fit it to my situation. I listened to the talk multiple times and finally found the secret: Every single dollar that comes into your possession must be assigned a purpose, *before* it is spent, not afterwards. I also came to realize that budgets never work properly unless you know exactly what your expenses are and can accurately predict what they should be in the future.

With this new insight, I spent a week opening a years' worth of mail and getting a realistic view of my actual financial situation. I analyzed several years' worth of bank statements and identified recurring expenses, utility billing trends and most importantly, over $15,000 worth of uncategorized spending per year that was the root cause of our financial problems. I then contacted a business coach who graciously agreed to take me under his wing in a mentorship role. We sat down and took an honest look at my finances. With his help, I confirmed that I was on the right track.

When I sat down with my coach, I was two months behind on my Mortgage and was facing cutoff by every one of my Utilities. Three months later, without significantly changing our family income, my wife and I had made five mortgage payments and had caught up on all our Utility bills. We then turned our focus to paying off the debts and putting money away for emergencies. It is significant how much stress is erased from your life when you gain control of your finances

My hope for you is that if you have been facing financial challenges, you will find something in this book that will help you to get your head out of the sand and take control of your personal finances. The information in this book is not theory. It is field-tested. Not every chapter in this book will apply to every person. I guarantee though, that if you follow the advice in this book, you will be able to reduce or eliminate the financial stress in your life and marriage, because you will now be in complete control of your finances with the resources to weather almost any storm.

Chapter 1
Preparing for the Storms

For years, when friends would ask how I was doing financially, I would say that I was treading water with my nose just barely sticking out above the surface. If you have been treading water or are near to drowning, more drastic action is needed. You need to get rid of excess weight that will drag you down. In the realm of personal finances, this extra weight is a combination of all the expenses and purchases you are making that are not part of your budget or spending plan.

This book is like a life ring I have thrown to you. Soon you will be swimming instead of treading water or drowning. Eventually you will be on the beach or floating on the water in a boat, instead of swimming in it. Before you can enjoy the beach or the boat, you first need to swim there. You will never make it unless you first ditch all the extra weight and have resources to deal with the storms of life.

Clinging to the Life Raft

Are you tired of living paycheck to paycheck with more month than money? If you need to spend $140 on a battery for your car, does it create a money crisis? Does it seem like every time you put $100 in your savings account; it is gone before the month is out? Are you and your spouse constantly arguing about money? It is hard to enjoy life if you are clinging to the life raft, knowing that one rogue wave will cause you to lose your grip and drown. If you are one of the millions of Americans who are living paycheck to paycheck, you need to make some drastic changes in your life. You have three alternatives-reduce your expenses, increase your income, or a combination of both. Increasing your income will not change your situation because your expenses will increase to match your new higher income unless you gain full control of your finances.

Some of you are living an extremely austere lifestyle because you are trying to save all your discretionary income for reaching a goal or you might be earning so little money that you have no choice but to cut all discretionary spending. When extra money does show up, it often gets spent immediately on buying all the things you were deprived of or just paying the creditors who call the most often. If you are in one of these situations, you really need to develop control over your finances so that when you do get an influx of money, you have a plan in place to work with it.

Many of my readers are just getting by. They work a job or two. They live from paycheck to paycheck with no money set aside for the storms of life. No matter what they do, they just can't seem to get ahead. They scratch their heads in disbelief when they do their taxes and see how much money they earned with nothing to show for it. If this is your situation, there is only one way to change it without increasing your income. You must give a purpose to every dollar in your control. You need to free up at least twenty percent of your income. This twenty percent is what you will use to catch up on all your bills, build up a cash reserve, pay off your debts and increase the quality of your life. The next chapter will help you identify which expenses can be eliminated to free up twenty percent.

When you start applying the strategies found in this book, money that was once spent on frivolous purchases will instead be available to pay off debts and build a cushion. As your debt disappears, more money will be available for savings and financing new business ventures or investments.

It might have taken you years to get into your current situation, but focus, effort and some sacrifice can change your financial situation in a remarkably short time. To make it happen, you must build financial buffers and have total awareness of your income and expenses. The remainder of this chapter will give strategies to eliminate unnecessary emergencies that can waste your money.

Avoid Unnecessary Emergencies

Have you ever looked at your bank balance a couple days before payday and breathed a sigh of relief because as far as you could tell you had enough money in the bank to last till payday? Then, **BAM!!!** Out the blue would come a charge to your account that you completely forgot about or have no idea where it came from. The next thing you know, you are racking up $35 Non-Sufficient Fund fees. This can be avoided by knowing the amount and billing date of every one of your recurring expenses and keeping track of all spending and bank balances daily. It can also be avoided by keeping a

5

cushion in your balance. Let's look at some ways to avoid unnecessary emergencies by providing a cushion for your finances.

Overdraft Account

Most banks and Credit Unions allow their customers to have an overdraft fund. This is a small line of credit, usually ranging from $200-$500 that can be drawn on if your account goes below zero. If you don't have one, you should apply for it. However, most people who have an overdraft account have used up most of their reserve and only have about $15 available (or whatever minimum payment the bank pulls each month from the primary account). It does you no good to have an overdraft account if you have used it all up. It should be there solely as a cushion against emergencies, not as a buffer against laziness. If you have an overdraft account, you need to pay off any balance as soon as possible. This will be your first line of defense against a rogue financial wave.

$1000 Emergency Fund

Proper planning can prevent many fiscal emergencies. Unfortunately, there will always be unexpected expenses and situations that can't be planned for. Maintaining an emergency fund of at least $1000 will turn most "emergencies" into a minor inconvenience. This fund is not meant for keeping your account from over drafting. It is solely to provide funding for emergency situations like car repair, plumbing repair, insurance deductibles and other unplanned expenses that must be paid but were not budgeted. A $1000 emergency fund should be a high priority and you should set a goal of having this fund in place as soon as possible.

Timely Payment of Bills

There is another way to develop a cushion against emergencies. Most of your monthly bills will allow you to go late without consequences (other than a late fee) if you pay the bill before the next one is due. This can lead to trouble if you are already running behind. However, if you are paying all your bills on or before the due date, and especially if you pay them as soon as they come out; you will have a time cushion of a month, if a major emergency happens to you. If you pay your bills on the billing date, you will now have a cushion of up to two months.

Start this process by catching up on all your bills so that when each new bill comes out, there is no "past due" amount. Then work towards paying each bill as soon as you receive it. If you are already behind on all your bills, this goal will probably take about two to three months to achieve.

Preventive Maintenance

Have you ever had a flat tire get worn out unevenly? Do the guys at the tire shop know you by name? Tires can cost between $50 and $200 per tire. A good tire should not need a replacement until the advertised mileage has been reached. If your alignment is off, the tires will wear unevenly, which drastically reduces the life of the tire. An alignment costs between $60 and $100. Failure to get your car aligned can cost you hundreds of dollars each year.

Another form of preventive maintenance is to keep the fluid levels (oil, anti-freeze, etc.) full. Failure to keep the coolant full can cause overheating and a blown head gasket. This is a very expensive repair. I recently replaced a blown head gasket on a Mustang one of my daughters had bought. Even though I did the work, it still cost around $700 to get the car running. It was bad. There was water in the cylinders and the head was warped. If I hadn't done the work, it would have cost between $1600 and $3000. All of this because the previous owner had allowed the engine to overheat.

Get oil changes on a regular basis or do them yourself. Check the condition of hoses and belts, making sure they aren't cracked or rotted. If you drive an older car, look at the suspension system of the car. You will often see torn boots, and other problems with the steering and suspension. Jack the car up and make sure there is no play in the wheels. Make sure that all the lug nuts are tight. I once totaled a car (well, the insurance company totaled it) because my front wheel came off when I was doing a U-turn. This could have been prevented if I had tightened the lug nuts. If you can't do these things, then have a mechanic do them for you. It is always cheaper to do preventive maintenance than to fix or replace a car.

In your home, have an HVAC technician do a seasonal checkup on your heating and air conditioning.

Have the pest control company come out to do a preventive treatment of your home. I am currently having to rebuild my shed because termites got into the wood. It would have been much less expensive to have the pest control guy come out and check for termites before they did their damage.

Fill Your Pantry

Don't go rush out and spend hundreds of dollars on food you don't need while you are behind on your bills, but it is important to stock up on food staples. Your goal should be to have at least one month of non-perishable food items that you normally use and one replacement for each food item that lasts more than a month. For example, if you go through a bag of rice every two months, you should have one extra bag on hand. Try to eliminate unnecessary items such as snacks from your groceries and use the savings to slowly stock up. You should plan on having a month of food on hand within several months. This provides another cushion for your family if you have an unexpected situation that is more than your $1000 emergency fund can handle.

Trimming the Fat

Much of what we will talk about involves cutting out unnecessary expenses so that you can free up money to use for debt reduction and building a cushion. You also may be wondering, "How long do I have to cut back so severely on my expenses?" You are trying to trim all the fat off your budget so that you can have money to work with. This is especially important if you have an irregular or variable income. You need to build a reserve for the dry spells. If you commit to changing your habits, you will shortly have your bills caught up, debts paid off and money sitting in the bank. That is when you can ease off your money diet and start to enjoy some of the old guilty pleasures again.

The danger you need to worry about is that after a while, you will start to slip on your money diet and slowly, but surely you will find yourself eating into the money that you had been enthusiastically setting aside. You need to check your balances and identify, classify, justify and modify your spending every day or at least once each week. At the end of every month you need to analyze your finances and see if you need to adjust your spending. I guarantee that you will.

Develop a Plan of Action

There will be a time investment to gain control of your finances, but once you have everything set up you should only need to spend about five minutes each day reviewing your finances. Some days will take more time, especially paydays, but the time invested will pay off quickly. It usually takes several months to stabilize a shaky financial situation. You should, however, see results within the first couple weeks if you dig in and decide to apply what you will learn.

Questions

1. Do you have a path to retirement?

   _____

2. Do you have a $1000 Emergency Fund?

   _____

3. What is the one thing you can do today to start your plan of action?

   _____

4. When was the last time you checked your bank balance? How often do you check your balance?

   _____

5. When was the last time you put 10% or more of your paycheck into a savings account?

   _____

Action Steps

Preventive Maintenance

Do these three things before the week is over.

1. Check the oil level in your car and if it's dirty or low, get an oil change or change the oil yourself.
2. Stop at a gas station and fill your tires to the proper inflation level.
3. Check the coolant level.

Fill Your Pantry

List three foods you can buy this week that will help build your food cushion (i.e. canned vegetables, dried milk, mashed potatoes, rice).

1._____

2._____

3._____

Check Your Finances

Do these three things before the week is over.
1. Check the balance of each bank account.
2. Check the status or balance of each retirement account.
3. Locate each current bill or statement for all your retirement, investment and bank accounts.

Chapter 2
Identify, Classify, Justify, Modify

This book will help you set up a budget that works, but it is not a book about budgeting. Instead it is a comprehensive guide on taking complete control of your finances. I have always found budgets to be either too simple or too complex. There are some complex budget spreadsheets that you can download for free. They are incredibly time consuming and don't address the problem of unbudgeted expenses or variable incomes. A basic budget is necessary to build a framework, but the amazing turn-around of my financial condition was accomplished not by setting up a budget, but by placing an iron grip on our family finances and eliminating all unnecessary expenses. In later chapters, I will help you develop strategies to track your finances and proactively manage your money flow and set up a basic budget. It all starts by ending your uncontrolled, undisciplined, and unplanned spending. Now that you have your head out of the sand, you need to shake the sand off.

Lighten the Load

When a ship at sea starts taking on water and is in danger of sinking, the crew will try to lighten the load. This idea is illustrated in the Book of Acts 27:1-44. The Author, Luke, relates the events that happened while he and the Apostle Paul were onboard a ship. Battered by storms, the crew feared they would be driven onto the rocky shore. In verses 18 and 19, Luke tells how the crew lightened the load. *"18 The next day, because we were violently battered by the storm, they began throwing the cargo overboard, 19 and on the third day they threw the ship's gear overboard with their own hands.* If you are being battered by a financial storm, lighten your load. Rid yourself of unnecessary expenses and lighten your financial burden.

Identify, Classify, Justify, Modify

Throughout this chapter, we will be applying the system of Identify, Classify, Justify, and Modify. This system can be applied to behavior patterns and finances. In this chapter, we will identify behaviors that cost you money, classify those behaviors, and attempt to justify them. If they can't be justified, they must be modified, reduced or eliminated.

Slam the Brakes on Unbudgeted Purchases

Stopping unbudgeted spending is one of the most important things that you can do if you want to end your financial misery. Everything in this book is aimed at helping you gain complete control of your finances to the point that you will be able to predict the future. Nothing in this book or any other personal finance book will change your financial condition unless you first stop any spending that has not been purposed, budgeted or planned. Each month you have a finite amount of money flowing into your financial basket. For most people, that basket is a leaking sieve. If you can plug the holes, the money will still be there when you need it. Later, you can convert your current impulse spending into a budget category or an allowance, but for now, you must stop all impulse purchases. What is impulse spending? It is any purchase that is unplanned or undisciplined. Habit spending happens when you make purchases based on a habit, like buying coffee and donuts.

Habit Spending

Let's look at an example of Habit Spending in an average person's daily life. In the morning, they rush out the door and head to work. On the way to work they stop at their favorite convenience store and get a cup of coffee, a breakfast sandwich and maybe an energy drink and a bottle of water or soda. They pull out their Debit or Credit card and pay anywhere from $2 to $12. Later, they take a lunch break and go to their favorite restaurant and pay anywhere between $6 and $15 for lunch. If they smoke, they also spend an average of $6 to $8 per day on cigarettes. Although it varies by person, on average they will spend about $20 per day in feeding themselves away from home. Based on twenty workdays per month, this adds up to $400 each month. How many bills could you pay with that $400?

Impromptu Impulse Spending

Impulse Spending usually happens when you see something that you don't normally buy as a habit, such as a candy bar or magazine and then add to your habit purchase. This type of Impulse Spending adds up quickly and is especially dangerous to someone who is trying to take control of their finances. Every store has items placed near the entrance and cash registers that are specifically aimed to induce Impulse Spending. Feel free to indulge in Impulse Spending when you are rich and famous. Until then, stop the Impulse Spending now. Do not purchase anything on the spur of the moment.

Delayed Impulse Spending

There is another type of Impulse Spending that can be very expensive: Delayed Impulse Spending. This happens when you think about something that you would like and immediately go to a store to get it. In your mind, you have convinced yourself that you need the item and you need it now. STOP!!! Ask yourself if this purchase is necessary. Call your spouse or a friend and ask them if they think this purchase is necessary. Decide whether it is truly a need or just something that you want. Take the time to look online and do price comparisons. Determine if the purpose you needed the item for could be taken care of with the resources you already have on hand. If you determine that it truly is necessary to buy the item, then try to wait a day and turn it into a planned purchase. This type of spending is unpredictable and budget wrecking.

Duplicate Spending

Have you ever searched everywhere for a tool and could not find it, so you ran to the store and bought a replacement? Then, a week later you found the missing tool. Duplicated spending is wasteful and a drain on your budget. It is caused by sloppiness and laziness and can be avoided by putting everything in its place and cleaning up after yourself. I have been very prone to this problem. Whenever I need a flat head screwdriver, I can only find Phillips screwdrivers and vice versa. Just last week, I needed to fix a leak in the pipe going to the upstairs water heater. I spent an hour looking for a tube cutter and ended up driving to the home improvement store to buy one. This was an emergency because the water heater was in the attic and it was dripping into our bedroom. The next day, I located two other tube cutters in my auto repair toolbox. Oops. Duplicate spending is a sign of laziness and sloppiness. You can't afford to indulge in it. If your tools are constantly scattered, get a toolbox or use the one you already have

Duplicate spending can also occur when you unnecessarily buy cosmetics, housewares, dustpans, comforters and anything else that you already have, but are not satisfied with or can't locate when you need it. Don't spend money on something that you already have. Take the time to find it and to put it away when you are done. One important exception to this is that you should always have duplicate car keys. It is much less expensive to make an extra key than to have to call a locksmith.

Stop the Addiction Spending

Addiction Spending is very difficult to manage. It includes spending on tobacco products, alcohol, drugs, lottery tickets, sports betting, gambling and less obvious things like coffee, soda, energy drinks and non-alcoholic eggnog. I added eggnog because I realized in writing this, that drinking a quart of eggnog each day of

December is probably an addiction. Except for lottery tickets and illegal drugs, I will not be telling you that you must go Cold Turkey and immediately stop your addiction. Instead, I would like to help you be in full control of yourself and your addictions. An addiction is an activity or habit that is difficult to stop indulging in. It is up to you to work on reducing your dependence on the addiction. In the meantime, we will look at the various types of addiction spending and either eliminate them or turn them into a planned and tightly controlled expense.

Tobacco, Alcohol and Drugs

If you smoke or use alcohol, I won't be giving you a lecture on the health benefits of quitting. Let's look at the financial side of your addiction. Depending on the State you live in, a pack of cigarettes can cost anywhere between $5 and $13. Assuming you are a Pack-a-Day smoker, you are spending between $150 and $360 each month. An average visit to a bar can cost between $15 and $50. If you want to gain control of your finances, you must bring these addictions under control.

Decide to reduce the number of cigarettes you smoke each day. When you reach a level that you can stick with, then start filling your empty packs with that number of cigarettes. Make sure you have easy access to only one pack each day. Use a permanent marker to note the day on each pack. You are now in control of your addiction and are reducing your expenses at the same time. Of course, there are other strategies for quitting like electronic cigarettes, nicotine gum and support groups. Use what works for you.

If you don't think you can stop smoking, then track your spending on tobacco for a complete week. Most tobacco users assume they are smoking one pack per day, but often are smoking up to ten packs each week. Get an honest account of how much you smoke each week. Separate the tobacco purchase from anything else you are buying at the same time. Keep the receipts and add up the cost. This weekly cost will now become a controlled expense that you can predict.

Although it is controversial, switching to vaping is probably the most effective way to quit smoking. There are some studies that question the safety of vaping, but there is no question about whether vaping is less dangerous or expensive. Vaping has helped many people to quit smoking, but it takes a decision to quit. Otherwise you will be vaping and smoking.

I'm constantly amazed at how many people routinely buy a case of beer every Friday and then complain about their finances. There are support groups like Alcoholics Anonymous that can help you if you are an Alcoholic. As a general guideline, if you aren't an alcoholic and want to control your drinking because of the financial implications, limit your yourself to one drink per session. If you must drink, make the case last a month, not a weekend. You must decide what is more important-being in control of your finances or allowing Alcohol to rule your life.

I am going to assume that most of my readers do not use illegal drugs. However, in many States, marijuana is now becoming legal at the State level. Marijuana can be expensive, and it conflicts with the goal of taking control of your life. You must decide what is more important-experiencing your high or taking control of your life and finances. Choose wisely. Marijuana use is not normally associated with becoming financially sound.

Caffeine

Caffeine is a legal drug that can cause health problems and loss of sleep. It is highly addictive and can cause a severe drain on your finances. I was addicted to caffeine to the point that I was drinking two 2-liter bottles every day of caffeinated soda. While writing this book, I decided that I had no excuse for the addiction and plenty of motivation to save my money. I still drink some caffeinated beverages, but now I have mostly switched to water. For the cost of two 2-liters of soda, I buy a case of bottled water. If you only drink caffeine occasionally, then it will carry a punch when you need it too. If you must have your caffeine kick, either make it at home or the office. Don't waste your money on high-end three or four name lattes. If you are feeling smug about buying a cup of coffee at the gas station each morning for $1.79, remember to add an expense item in your budget for the $35.80 you are spending each month.

If you are meeting someone for business over a cup of coffee, try to go somewhere that has the "Never-empty Pot of Coffee". Don't try to impress your prospect with your knowledge of fancy high-end coffees and your ability to pay $15 plus tip. The IRS agent won't be amused when you try to explain why you tried to claim it on your taxes. Make sure to include the coffee as a budget item if you will be meeting with prospects or clients often. Keep in mind that just because you are meeting someone "over a cup of coffee" doesn't have to mean that you buy coffee. Get them a cup of coffee and yourself a water.

Lottery and Sports Betting

Playing the Lottery is addictive and extremely wasteful. The lottery has been described as a tax on the poor. The chances of winning more than you spend are extremely poor and every dollar spent on a ticket is a dollar that could have been used to gain control of your finances. Just stop buying them.

Sports betting is fun and addictive but is always a losing proposition. You may occasionally get a payoff, but sports betting has no place in the life of someone who is working to gain control of their finances. Fantasy leagues fall into this same category. They are time-consuming and can end up costing a lot of money. If you must indulge in a Fantasy League, then be sure to stick to a budget and keep it under control. Ask yourself if that money wouldn't be better spent on a bill.

Entertainment Spending

Let's revisit the illustration I use of treading water versus sitting on the beach or boat. Imagine you have fallen out of a boat and are left behind. You have the latest water-resistant phone. Are you going to get on the phone and call for help, or will you play the latest game you downloaded? Are you going to check out the movie lineup at the cineplex or get to business and start swimming? This example may seem ridiculous, but why then do you feel justified in spending money on Entertainment when you can't pay your past due Electric bill or put money in the offering plate? Excessive Entertainment Spending when you are having financial difficulties is an escape mechanism. You have your head in the sand and are trying to pretend you are not in trouble. you need to decide what is more important-Entertainment or Financial Stability.

Books and Magazines

I am an avid reader and read an average of five books each week. For me, reading is an addiction. My phone holds over four hundred eBooks, almost all of them Fiction. Since I have read all of them at least twice, I often make purchases of new books. This is an addiction that I had to bring under control because not only was I spending over $100 each month on books, but I was reading Fantasy and Science Fiction instead of the much harder Self-Improvement books. If you recognize yourself as a book addict, decide about how much you can afford to spend on new reading material and then make Books a budget category. Resolve not to buy any books that take you past this new limit you have set. You may also want to consider using Amazon or E-bay to sell books you are finished with. Do you have a complete set of First Print Star Trek books like I do? Maybe you can pay off a pesky bill with the proceeds from your book sales.

You may also want to do what I did. I made a conscious decision to take a long break from reading fiction and turned to non-fiction. I am reading an average of three success-oriented books every week as well as one spiritually-oriented book each week. If you are going to spend money on books, get books that will help you to enjoy success in all areas of your life. Instead of losing yourself in a book that will not make a positive impact on your life, read at least 15 minutes a day from a good success-oriented book. Learn to go to the library and borrow a book instead of always having to have the latest book on the day it is published. Many libraries will order a book if you request a title they don't have. After you've read several success books, read your favorite fiction book as a reward for a job well done

Cinema

Going to the Cinema to see a movie can be a fun way to spend time with a loved one or friend. It becomes addictive spending when the attendants know you by name and you have a favorite seat in each viewing room. Until your finances are under control, you need to severely restrict the number of movies you attend each week. Try to limit yourself to one or two movies each month. Better yet, wait till the movie comes out on DVD or Netflix. Let's assume that your movie ticket costs $7.00 and the refreshments cost $13. If you take your spouse or loved one, you will spend $40. One movie per week will cost you $160 per month. If you must watch multiple movies, then stop visiting the refreshment stand. Can you really afford to eat the overpriced popcorn when your electricity is getting ready to be cut off? Try going during Matinee hours. Look for discounted showings. Better yet, wait till all your bills are caught up and current. On that happy occasion, take your spouse to the theater as a celebration.

Movies Channels and Services

Closely related to Cinema are Premium Movie channels, Redbox, DVD purchases and Apps like Netflix and Hulu. My advice is to immediately call your cable provider and cancel any premium movie subscriptions. Don't purchase any DVD or Blu-ray discs unless it is a movie that you anticipate watching multiple times. It is not uncommon for a recently released movie to cost over $20. Redbox may seem less expensive, but if you don't return it on time, the movie will have daily late fees. It is also difficult to budget due to the varying costs of each rental. Netflix or Hulu are good alternatives, but it can be costly if you have multiple viewing services. Pick one and cancel the others.

Phone Apps, Music Services and Games

If you go to the Google or Apple store, there are thousands of Apps and games that can "nickel and dime" you to death. Try using the free version of an app before purchasing the premium version. It is always frustrating to spend money on an app only to find out that it doesn't perform the way you expect. If you must play games on your phone, try to stick to the free ones. Phone Apps are almost impossible to budget because the price varies so widely. Take a break on buying new apps unless you have a critical need for one that you can't find a free version to use. Don't spend money on duplicate movie or music Apps and Services.

Sports

I'm getting ready to hit a sore spot for many people. We already discussed Sports betting and Fantasy League. Now we are going to discuss Sports Spending If you are going to the games, you can easily spend hundreds of dollars each month for the tickets. If you are going to a sports bar, your bill could easily be $20-$30 per person. Recently, it has become much easier to watch the games online or even on your phone. Examine the different costs of your sports viewing and settle on the least expensive one.

Take Control of Your Food Budget

After Housing and Utility expenses, Groceries are often the largest portion of the average family's budget. There are many strategies out there to cut down on your food budget. There are some hidden traps in many of the strategies. In general, you should make a grocery list based on a weekly menu plan and stick to it. Avoid impulse buying while going through the aisles. Just because it is on sale doesn't mean you need to buy it. Try to make one trip to the store in which you buy the items on your list. If you need to make a quick trip to the store for milk or other perishables, make a list and stick to it. Don't forget to add breakfast and lunch items to help eliminate those expensive visits to convenience stores and restaurants.

The goal of cutting costs in your grocery shopping is not to get more food for the same amount of money. The goal is to get the same amount of food for less money and use the freed-up money to gradually stock up your pantry and then augment other parts of your budget.

Store Sales

Stores constantly have sales. Your goal is not necessarily to get food at the cheapest price possible. Instead, you are setting a limit on your spending and only buying the food that is necessary to meet your menu planning for the week. Keep on the lookout for sales on items you use often. Don't buy an item that is on sale unless it's part of your grocery list or is so low priced that it needs to be on your list.

Coupons and Rebates

Coupons can be a great tool for saving money. A careful coupon user can save hundreds of dollars each year by using coupons. Most coupons are for Brand Name products. Check to be sure that the price after using the coupon is comparable to the Store Brand price. Avoid using coupons for items you don't actually need.

Be careful about buying something because of a rebate. Unless it is an instant rebate, there will often be conditions that make it difficult to get your money back. Companies that offer rebates expect a large percentage of their customers to never actually mail in their rebate.

Ask yourself this question: when was the last time you received money from a mail in rebate?

Bulk Buying

Wholesale clubs can save money over the long haul if used carefully. Until you have complete control of your finances, I would recommend not buying food and other household items in bulk unless you normally buy large quantities of the item. It is very easy to make an impulse buy at a Wholesale Club. Unless you are trying to stock up your underground fallout shelter, you probably don't need a year's worth of toilet paper.

Eating Out and Ordering Delivery

Cut down severely the number of times you and your family eat out or order delivery. It is always less expensive to make your own food. You can buy premium steak, asparagus and dessert for the entire family for less than the cost of the average Pizza delivery order. I am not saying that you can never order Pizza or go out to eat, but during this initial phase when you are trying to get control of your finances, make eating out and ordering delivery a special occasion.

I delivered Pizza off and on for over twenty years. I was always amazed at how I could take two deliveries and see such a huge difference between what the customers were paying. I have delivered two pizzas that cost over $40 (not including tip) to one customer and then deliver two pizzas, breadsticks and a dessert to another customer for less than $25. What made the difference in price? One customer ordered online or called the store and placed an order for exactly what they wanted. The other customer asked for and carefully compared the current specials. They also took advantage of the Customer Appreciation program which gives credit towards purchases of future pizza. You can save even more money by getting carryout instead of delivery.

SUGAR BEAR, INSTEAD OF ORDERING PIZZA, HOW ABOUT TAKING A WALK TO THE SANDWICH SHOP?

Eating out can be extremely expensive. If you are used to taking the family out for dinner after church on Sunday, you probably spend close to $70. You need to do something different. Start a tradition of having a big family meal at home on Sunday afternoon. This would be an example of modifying an expense.

I always keep my eyes out for meat bargains at the grocery store. Last week, for the cost of two pizzas, I bought three hams for $.49/lb. They were originally marked at over $20 per ham. I got them for around $7 each. We had a very nice Sunday dinner with one and made a rice and ham casserole with the left overs. Then, two weeks later, we did it again. For years, I fed our family of six with a grocery budget of around $100 per week. Take a good look at the receipt from your next shopping trip. Can you make any changes? Try to plan your meals and center them on items you already have. Groceries should be a major focus of your budget trimming efforts.

Keep All Receipts

Later in this book I will discuss strategies for tracking your expenses and gaining control. Starting today, keep every single receipt for every purchase you make. There are phone apps that allow you to take a picture of a receipt and turn it into a PDF. Also, some finance software programs like Quicken allow you to attach a photo of a receipt to a transaction. Either way, it is important to keep all receipts in either paper or electronic form. Before you can control your finances, you must learn how to track and analyze them. Start now! It is impossible to track and categorize your cash spending without keeping receipts.

If you are making a purchase that includes several categories of spending, try to split the purchase into two separate transactions. As an example, if you stop for gas, but also buy a breakfast sandwich, pay for them separately and get both receipts. Either file the receipt or take a picture of it the same day as the purchase. The receipt does you no good if it is on the floor of your car. It is especially critical to keep your receipts or have electronic copies of them if you are self-employed or own a small business.

Don't Be a Hypocrite

Some of you will get very excited about the ideas you find here and then will lay down the law with your spouse. Don't get on your spouse's case if she buys a tube of lipstick, especially if you just spent $10 at the Chinese restaurant instead of packing a lunch. The ideas in this book will work best if both partners are working on them together. If you aren't getting cooperation from your spouse, then lead by example. Most likely you are half of the problem. If you fix half the problem, you are more than halfway there. If, however, your spouse is spending all the money you are saving, you need to sit down and talk it over. Give them this book to read or read it together. Don't get into an argument about it.

Non-Sufficient Fund (NSF) Fees

One of the worst ways to have money leak out of your household money basket is to overdraw your bank account and be charged an NSF fee. These fees usually range from $25 - $35. I have had situations when I tried to purchase an item and my debit card was declined. The store clerk helpfully would suggest that I try to use Credit. I would then go home, log into my bank account and find out that I was now overdrawn. Then the phone insurance, music service, on-hold credit purchases, etc. would start showing up. My bank would very helpfully pay each item and charge me $35 for the privilege. This would often happen the day before payday. Several times I found myself with a negative balance of more than $400! All of this was because I did not keep diligent track of my bank balance. I had my head in the sand. In the rest of the book you will learn how to know exactly what your balance is and will be. For now, log in at least daily so that you can avoid the pain of losing so much money for nothing in return.

Check to see if your bank will email low balance alerts. You can set an amount that will trigger an alert. Make sure you match this to the buffer amount you have for each account. This could be $100 at first and then later, $1000. NSF Fees can also be avoided if you have an overdraft account with money in it.

Avoid Purchasing High Ticket Items

Some of my readers have already conquered their habit and impulse spending. My brother Kevin, who is an Accountant, pointed out that some people have financial difficulties due to making too many high-ticket purchases. This problem often occurs because they know they have surplus money sitting in their savings or checking account or they have just enough credit to be able to buy it.

High Income Earners and people who are already on some form of a budget are prone to make unnecessary high-ticket item purchases. Hold off on that new boat, sports car or 90" TV until you have six months of expenses sitting in the bank AND you can afford to pay cash for the item without using your savings.

I fell into this trap over twenty-five years ago and am still feeling the effects of it. I wanted to buy a conversion van with all the bells and whistles. I was very determined to get it, so when the financing fell through for a new van, I prayed about it and decided that if the financing for a used van went through that it would be God's will (I figured out later that God doesn't work that way). I had just gotten a new job that paid over $3000/month. That would be equivalent to about $5000/month now. The financing went through on a $30,000 used conversion van. The payments were $900/month, but I thought I could afford it. Three weeks after I purchased the van, the company I had started working for closed its doors. Can anyone say Bankruptcy?

Don't think that just because you earn a six-figure income you are immune to the problems I described above. What will happen to you if you purchase a fancy car, a beach home or a boat and then your company is bought out and you are sending out resumes in hopes of getting a job before your house of cards comes crashing down. Future income is never a substitute for cash in the bank. Never make a purchase decision based on current or future income.

Purchase decisions should always be based on current cash reserves, NOT on current or future income. Something is only affordable if you can pay cash for it, not if you can make the payments on it.

I strongly suggest having a mentor who will hold you accountable to your budget. I had access to a mentor at that time who taught the following guidelines:

1. Never make a major purchase without checking with your mentor or coach.
2. Never use credit to pay for something (other than a house) unless you can afford to pay cash for it.

3. If your business gives you a dream, let the business pay for the dream.

If I had taken my mentor's teaching to heart, I would have had a much different financial situation over the past twenty years. You better believe that now I follow these guidelines as if my life depends on it.

Avoid All High Interest Loans

When you face having your Electricity shut off or your car repossessed, it is very tempting to get a payday loan or some other type of high interest loan. Within 3 miles of my house you can find five Car Title loans, ten Payday or "No Credit Needed" loan places, and five Pawn Shops. At one point, I had a title loan, pawn loan and payday loan at the same time.

I should probably put a red box around this whole section and capitalize every word in red letters. These places are TRAPS!!! They will kill you financially. A typical $500 loan will cost you over $900 if you pay it on time. If you currently are stuck in one of these loans, make it a high priority to pay it off as quickly as possible once you have caught up with your bills. Make sure to account for any of these loans when you list your expenses.

Be Careful About Loaning Money

I am the mentor for a young man who is ambitious and hard working. He was doing okay until he made a loan to a family friend who would have been evicted unless someone helped him. Now he is struggling because he has no cushion- he threw it away on a loan. It is difficult to see someone you love, deal with hard times. You are not a bank. I'm not saying you can't help a friend or family member, but don't loan them money. It would be better to just give it to them.

There are exceptions, of course. I would have been in an extremely bad situation several years ago, if my friend had not helped me out. I was facing having both my water and electricity turned off. I could pay the water, but not the electricity which was over $1000. He paid my bill and allowed me to work off the money I owed him. This same friend also loaned me money when I was faced with losing my house. I believe that the reason he loaned me the money was because I humbled myself and asked him to be my mentor. Without his guidance, I would not have started down the path to financial control.

If you don't have the equivalent of six months of expenses sitting in the bank, you are not financially sound enough to loan money to people. This may seem harsh, but you are not a bank or payday loan company. One last thought. Don't loan money to anyone you aren't mentoring unless you can afford to lose both the money and the friendship. If you are mentoring someone, think long and hard before loaning money to the person you are mentoring. It can be heartbreaking watching someone you are mentoring go through difficult financial situations. You aren't there to bail them out when they mess up. You are there to help them figure out a solution to their problem, not be the temporary solution.

Vacations

A friend of mine from Church reminded me that vacations are for making memories. This is true, and many people scrimp and save all year, so they can spend several thousand dollars for a trip to Disney or a cruise to the Bahamas or a tour of Europe. This is fine, and every family should experience at least one major vacation before the kids all leave the house. If, however, you are doing this each year and are using the money that should be going into your savings, you need to give this some thought. Studies suggest that expensive vacations cause stress because the vacationers feel pressured to get their money's worth

In contrast, a weekend at a campground would cost less than $200, including a new tent. The pictures of your children running away from the skunk will be priceless. Find out what museums, parks, recreation areas and historical sites are in your state. Many of these attractions are free, or low cost. You will make many more memories spending $200 per month on weekend getaways than you will on one vacation that costs thousands of dollars. Stick with the free attractions until you have built up a buffer in your finances. Then start adding the getaways. When it comes time to set goals, get pictures of your dream vacation and put them on your refrigerator. When possible, try to combine business with vacation. If you and your spouse go out of town to attend a conference, take time to visit a museum or other local attraction.

The Free Vacation Trap

There are multiple companies out there who are just dying to give you an "all-expenses paid" or "4 night get-away" at your choice of location. They will even give you a free cruise if you show up and sit through their presentation. Savvy consumers often use this as a means of saving money on vacations. If you are going to sign up, especially if they want you to pay for the privilege, be ready to read the fine print and endure the well-trained sales person who is going to put extreme pressure on you to buy their product or sign up for their time-share. I would strongly suggest that you avoid these situations while you are gaining control of your finances. There truly is no such thing as a free vacation. At the very least, you will have to pay the taxes. Don't believe me? Read the fine print or the IRS agent will read it to you.

What to Do with the Extra Money

Be careful not to go spending the money that you will free up following the advice in this chapter. Later chapters will go into greater detail about how to use this extra money, but for now, let it build up in your bank account until you have developed a budget or spending plan. There are a couple of important exceptions to this guideline.

The first exception is for those of you who have been unable to give to your church or favorite charity. It is important to make giving a priority in your life. If you have been unable to give regularly because you haven't had control of your finances, start giving at least 10% of the money you are freeing up. The goal is to give away 10% of your total income, but that should wait until you have brought all your utility bills and rent/mortgage up to date. However, if the money you are freeing up exceeds 10% of your income, you should consider starting the giving immediately. Check with your mentor or someone you trust who is in a position of leadership at your place of worship if you are unsure of how much to give.

Another exception applies when you have a past due Rent or Mortgage payment, or a soon to be shut off Utility such as Water, Gas or Electricity. Go ahead and use the freed-up money to pay the obligation. Do not use the freed-up money to pay off loans or credit cards now. Catch them up if they are late, but don't get tempted to pay them off early just yet. Wait until you have developed a plan. It is important to first pay any past due balances on your utility bills.

If you are unsure if you should spend some of the freed-up money on bills or use it to build up a surplus, check with your mentor. At this point it is important to have a cushion. You want to always have several hundred dollars in your bank account. This will help you avoid paying NSF charges and will eliminate a lot of the stress.

If you are currently working more than two jobs, you need to consider the possibility of eliminating the one that provides the least amount of income. Chances are it is a minimum wage job providing less than a couple hundred dollars per month. Ask the Supervisor of your second higher paying job if you could increase your hours. Trying to juggle three jobs is extremely stressful. If you must have a third job, consider choosing a job that produces tips. Chances are, the extra job was being used to pay for all the unnecessary spending and is no longer necessary.

Consider Adding More Income

I know that I just recommended avoiding too many jobs. However, if you are so far behind in your bills that even eliminating all your extra expenses doesn't leave you with any freed-up money, you need to consider adding another job. If you have evenings free, you might want to consider a delivery job. The hours are flexible, and you can usually count on bringing home about $60 or more each evening from tips. The tip money would help to cover expenses like gas, groceries and miscellaneous expenses that are hard to budget and predict. Delivering pizza for several months could be exactly what you need to catch up on all your past due bills.

There are many other ways to add short-term income. Consider renting the empty room to a college student. Turn your hobby into an income producer. Sell unused books or musical instruments on Amazon and E-Bay. Sell custom T-Shirts on a website. Set up a table at the flea market. Tutor a student or give instrument lessons. Buy a "mechanics special" car and then fix it and sell it. Put a plow on your truck if you live in the North. Babysit children so their parents have an alternative to day care. Develop an idea and run with it.

You may want to consider starting a home-based or network marketing business once you have control of your finances. I highly approve of having alternate forms of income, especially if the opportunity has a mentorship system in place. From personal experience, I can tell you that you will never make any significant money in any business unless you have control of your finances and have a mentor. Any business, traditional or otherwise, needs an investment of time and money to make it work. There must also be a system for success in place with examples of success you can emulate.

If you are currently living paycheck to paycheck with little or no savings, it may take several months to be in a position where you can safely redirect your freed-up money to investing in an opportunity. If it is a good business opportunity, your mentor would rather spend several months helping you gain control of your finances than getting you started too quickly and watching you fail. There is a reason why many restaurant franchises cost over $250,000. The Franchiser wants to make sure the new franchisee has the resources available for success. The same principle applies for a home-based business. You will likely fail if you don't have resources available, though you will rarely need more money than you are likely to free up by cutting your expenses. Once you have mastered your finances, you are highly likely to succeed in any legitimate opportunity that comes your way. It all starts with a conscious decision to take control of your finances and have a purpose for every dollar that comes into your possession.

An Important Beginning

If you follow the guidelines you have just read, you will start to see immediate results. Be creative. There are many ways to cut down on your expenses. Later, when you have thousands of dollars in the bank, you can buy the latest doodad and increase spending on impulse buying. You must decide now. If you want the peace of mind that comes from having total control of your finances, you must eliminate all undisciplined, unplanned, unnecessary and unwise spending. The rest of the book will show you how to use the money that has been freed up to become current on all your bills and start the path to being debt-free and in total control of your personal finances.

Action Steps
Examine Your Spending

List spending behaviors you can change or modify immediately. Start looking for ways to save money. Be creative.

1. _____

2. _____

Modify Your Entertainment Spending

Identify three forms of entertainment you and your spouse regularly spend money on. Write down a possible alternative.

1._____   _____

2._____   _____

Identify Your Spending

Find last month's bank statement and start looking at each entry that is a purchase. Try to identify the purpose of each transaction. Don't worry about recurring expenses like utility bills. We will deal with them in the next chapter. List two transactions that surprised you when you identified them.

1. _____

2. _____

Classify Your Spending

After you have identified each purpose, try to classify it. Is it a gasoline purchase or perhaps a habit purchase? For now, just write the classification right on the statement or printout. List two transactions that you couldn't classify because you can't remember what you purchased.

1. _____

2. _____

Justify Your Spending

After you have identified and classified each purchase, try to justify it. Was it necessary? Could you have bought something less expensive? Was it bought on impulse? List two transactions that you could not justify.

1. _____

3. _____

Modify Your Unjustified Spending

If you are not able to justify a purchase, you must modify or eliminate it. List two transactions that need to be dealt with.

1. _____

2. _____

Chapter 3
Learning to Swim

In the previous chapters, I showed you how to stop drowning in your expenses and start treading water consistently. The problem with treading water is that you have no protection from the waves of life. If an emergency such as a blown car engine or a loss of income happens, you will be struggling to avoid being drowned. The steps in this chapter are the beginning steps and temporary measures that will allow you to begin taking control of your finances while you learn to swim. Since you are probably already in the deep end, it is important to learn to ride the waves. In the rest of the book I will be teaching you how to swim and ride the waves.

Find a Mentor

It is important to find a Mentor. Look for someone you know who is in control of their finances and ask if they would be willing to spend time helping you to gain control of your life. A mentor will help you avoid dead ends and can give personal examples that will save you time and money. Your mentor will see your blind spots and most importantly can be used for accountability. Having someone take a personal interest in you can make the difference in success or failure. Be accountable to your spouse and a mentor. Remember, they can only give you good advice if you give good and complete information. If you are holding out pertinent information, the advice will be flawed.

Set Up a Temporary Allowance

In Chapter Two, I showed several ways to eliminate or reduce habit, addictive and impulse purchases. Now, make an educated guess of how much money you and your spouse need for weekly spending on things such as gas and lunch. Also, make a good guess of how much you spend on addictive or habit spending. Be honest with yourself and your spouse. If you spend $30 each week on tobacco or caffeine, include that spending in the total until you can eliminate the unnecessary spending. It might be $50 per week for you and $75 per week for your spouse. Draw this money out of your bank and put it into two (or if you are single, one) envelopes. Write "Allowance" in the center-top and then underneath write out the dollar amount. This is the only money you should allow yourselves to access for personal discretionary use.

Later in the setup process, you will refine the allowance amounts based on an analysis of your spending. Eventually you will be able to increase the amount of allowance which can be used for indulging in the occasional guilty pleasure. If you or your spouse is a cash-oholic it will be important to write down each purchase on the envelopes and keep your receipts until you have converted the allowance into an account in your finance software.

If your spouse earns more money than you, it is important to have them be part of the decision-making process. They may feel taken advantage of, if they don't understand why you are limiting how much they can spend. Make sure they understand that the amount of the allowance will change in a few weeks after you evaluate your spending. Don't argue over this. If your spouse says he or she needs more money, then modify the allowance. At this point, the allowance should cover only the necessities like gas, personal care items and meals, if they aren't able to bring lunch to work. Later, the allowance will be modified to include a bit of mad money. At this stage, it is critical to keep all receipts.

Wean Yourself Away from Credit Cards

IMHO (In my humble opinion) no one needs more than one credit card. Some very disciplined people charge recurring expenses to their card and faithfully pay off their card each month. In doing so, they earn flight points and other "benefits" that make it worth taking advantage of.

Most people who use credit cards have too many cards and not enough discipline. They are carrying thousands of dollars of debt on five or more cards. They also have store charge cards for multiple Department Stores, Hardware Stores and Wholesale Buying Clubs. It is not uncommon for someone to make payments to ten or more charge cards each month. They are drowning in Credit Card Debt.

I know many people who buy their groceries, gas, garden tools, meals at restaurants and just about everything else on their cards. They are fooled into thinking that 1% Cash Back on their purchases makes up for the 15-30% interest on their purchases if they don't pay off the full balance each month. If I am describing you, please stop using ALL your credit cards for anything other than recurring expenses. If you have a card that has a good interest rate and you are earning travel and hotel points, only use it for bills that you have the funds to pay each month. All other purchases should now be made with a debit card or cash.

Make a Temporary Budget

Use an Excel spreadsheet to make a temporary budget. I call it temporary, because your final budget will have many additions and changes. You can download Libre Office or Open Office for no cost and use the included spreadsheet program if you don't have Microsoft Excel. If you are old school, you can get a piece of paper and a calculator and do this by hand. Download the Temporary Budget spreadsheet or PDF budget from my website at www.gyhootsbook.com to make this process easier. The website also contains instructions for building your own spreadsheets. If your mentor has a budget sheet they like to work with, then use it. By now you should have an idea of your monthly expenses and income. Now is the time to set them down

Don't worry about perfection at this point. You are trying to get started. There is a reason that I call this a temporary budget. Your temporary monthly budget should look something like the following example:

Temporary Budget

Net Income	Monthly	Weekly
Bob Salary	$4,200	$1,050
Sally Paycheck	$600	$150
Sally Tip Income	$1,200	$300
Total Net Income	$6,000	$1,500

Expenses	Monthly	Weekly
Tithes	$600	$150
Mortgage or Rent	$1,300	$325
Groceries	$500	$125
Household	$200	$50
Electricity	$300	$75
Water	$100	$25
Natural Gas	$150	$38
Internet/Cable	$120	$30
Cell Phone	$150	$38
Car payment	$300	$75
Car Insurance	$220	$55
Gas	$240	$60
Bob Allowance	$200	$50
Sally Allowance	$300	$75
Credit Card Payments	$300	$75
Medical Bills	$100	$25
Student Loan Payments	$220	$55
Miscellaneous	$800	$200
Total Expenses	$5,500	$1,375

	Monthly	Weekly
Target Amount (20%)	$1,200	$300
Freed Up Money	$500	$125

If the amount in the Freed-Up Money line is a positive number, you have money to work with. You will use this to build a reserve, catch up on past due bills,

47

reduce your debt and start building an asset. If the number is negative, then you need to prioritize the expenses and pay the most critical bills first. You will need to carefully analyze all your expenses and find ways to reduce them.

In the Temporary Budget example, Bob and Sally have an estimated monthly income of $6000 and expenses totaling $5500. On paper, they currently have an estimated $500 per month freed up. Their goal is to free up $1200 (20%) each month. They need to target the miscellaneous expenses and allowances because the $125 per week they currently have freed up is probably disappearing before the week is over.

Look at the Weekly column. Many people have periods of draught in their finances because they didn't designate money on a weekly basis to pay large monthly bills. In the above example, if Bob and Sally set aside $325 each week for their mortgage, they won't have to use most of one paycheck to pay it. The money will be sitting there waiting to be used. A good place to set this money aside would be a savings account attached to the bank account you pay your bills from. The money is there, waiting to be used, but not part of the daily picture.

Have you ever had to list your various monthly expenses on a credit application? Most likely you made some wild guesses at what you spent because you really had no clue how much you spend on groceries, insurance, etc. This is what you are going to do now. Enter the monthly net incomes (after taxes) for both you and your spouse. Next, enter the names and estimated amounts of the recurring monthly expenses you know about. Enter the correct amounts if you know them. The Weekly column will be automatically calculated.

Keep in mind that your temporary budget will change. As you go through the following sections, you will identify recurring expenses that need to be added to the budget. If you start getting too many recurring expenses, try combining them as single entries on the budget. Have one entry for utilities and another for all debt reduction etc.

Get an Accurate Picture of Your Finances

Make or Download a Spreadsheet

One of the secrets to my method of gaining complete control of your finances is knowing the billing and due dates for every one of your recurring bills. Before I got my head out of the sand, there were too many times that my Water and other utilities were cut off because I had the money but didn't realize that the cut-off date was approaching. This problem was solved when I started

49

opening my mail and recording the due dates of all my bills.

One of the reasons for using a spreadsheet is to be able to see in a glance when your bills are issued and when they are due. You will fill it with the billing and due dates of each of your Utility bills and other monthly payments like loans and credit cards. I would recommend visiting my website at www.gyhootsbook.com where you can download the Financial Picture spreadsheet. It has three sheets, Monthly Bill Information, Recurring Expenses and Debt. The spreadsheets and PDF files on the book website are compatible with smartphones that have Microsoft Excel and Adobe PDF apps installed.

Make a Bills Directory on Your Computer

The next step is to make directory and sub-directories on your computer or cloud storage. A backup should be made of these directories on a flash drive which you will update at least once a month. These directories will hold either scans or downloads of all your statements. I would recommend downloading at least a year's worth of statements from each of your Utilities, Insurance Companies and any other account that allows downloads of your statements. If you are not able to download the statements, you will need to scan or take pictures of each statement and upload them to the proper directory.

Name	Date modified	Type
Electricity	1/26/2017 3:11 PM	File folder
Water	1/26/2017 3:11 PM	File folder
Natural Gas	1/26/2017 3:12 PM	File folder
Cell Phone	1/26/2017 3:12 PM	File folder
Car Insurance	1/26/2017 3:12 PM	File folder
Medical Bills	1/26/2017 3:12 PM	File folder
Credit Card	1/26/2017 3:13 PM	File folder

As you download the bills, name them in a consistent manner using the name of the bill and the billing date.

Power Bill 1-5-16	3/31/2016 11:30 AM	Adobe Acrobat D...
Power Bill 2-3-16	3/31/2016 11:31 AM	Adobe Acrobat D...
Power Bill 3-3-16	3/21/2016 6:21 AM	Adobe Acrobat D...
Power Bill 3-4-15	10/27/2015 6:50 AM	Adobe Acrobat D...

For each account, when you open the first statement, copy the Account Number, billing date, due date, website, phone number into the Monthly Bill Information sheet.

Monthly Bill Information

Expense	Account #	Phone Numb	Website User Name	Website Password	Bill Day	Due Day
Wise Owl Wireless	111111111111111	(800) 555-5555	UserName	GYHoots$24$7	4	28

Then, for each statement, enter the amount due (not the past due) into the appropriate Month column in the Recurring Expenses Sheet.

Expense	Jan	Feb	Mar	April	May
Wise Owl Cellular	$144.33	$155.00	$155.00	$151.00	$177.00
Windy Plain Electric	$544.33	$622.12	$433.22	$334.23	$230.22

Expense	Jan	Feb	Mar	April	May	Jun	Jul	Aug	Sep	Nov	Dec	Average
Wise Owl Cellular	$144.33	$155.00	$155.00	$151.00	$177.00	$177.00	$155.00	$155.00	$144.43	$145.54	$144.76	$142.01
Windy Plain Electric	$544.33	$622.12	$433.22	$334.23	$230.22	$223.66	$217.10	$199.34	$270.45	$403.20	$522.98	$333.40

You will notice that some bills, such as electricity vary widely in cost, depending on usage. If you look back at the past year's billing, you can make a good prediction of future usage and costs. Enter the amount due for each month based on the month from the previous year.

There is a nifty little trick you can use on the spreadsheet to make accessing each account website easier. Highlight the cell that has the name of the Utility or Company. Press the Control Key and the letter K (Control-K). This brings up the hyperlink window. Go to the log in page of the account and paste the web address into the Address field.

Paste the address into the address bar and press **OK**. Now if you want to visit the site, you can click on the name of the account and the website will open. Your user name and passwords are all in one location. If you keep your passwords here, you should protect the worksheet. You can do this by going to File>Info>Protect Workbook and choose the Encrypt with Password Option.

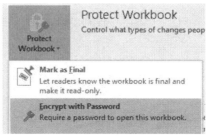

Gather Your Mail

I hope that you are not like I was when it comes to mail. I would ignore any mail that would remind me of my sad financial condition. When I decided to get my head out of the sand, I gathered the piles of mail from various locations in my house (including the bottom dresser drawer) and started to open my mail. I was embarrassed to find that many of the letters and bills were over a year old. I was also rather upset when I opened a letter that contained a sizeable refund check from one of my Utility companies that had expired.

Start Opening the Mail

What I want you to do now, is to get a trash bag and sort through all the mail. Throw out any obvious junk mail, credit card applications, donation requests and advertising. Now go through the pile again. Don't open anything now but start making piles for each category. You will need a large space for this, like the spare bed or the floor. All medical bills go in one pile, bank statements go in another, utility bills in another and so forth. Make separate piles for mail that needs to be read but is not a bill and for envelopes that don't identify the sender.

Monthly Bills and Utilities

Start with your Utility bills. Divide the Utilities pile into separate piles for each Utility. Open a letter from each Utility. If the letter is a shut-off notice, throw it away (unless it is current). and open another one. If you have already downloaded your bills, you can throw each bill away after confirming you have an electronic version, or you can file them in a filing cabinet. If you haven't downloaded the statements, locate the billing date, date due, Account Number, phone number and website address. Enter the Name of the Utility and the post and due dates into the spreadsheet. Scan or take a picture of each statement. Now you can throw away or file each bill. Repeat this process for all Utilities.

Now do the same thing to any other monthly bills you receive statements for. This could be Insurance, credit payments such as Car Loans, Credit Card Statements and any other monthly bill. Enter the information we talked about earlier. Most companies are consistent on the billing and due dates. You will be adding to this list of bills when you analyze your bank statements, but for now, you have a reference that will tell you at a glance all the important information about each bill.

	A	B	C	D	E	F	G
1	Account Information						
2	Expense	Account #	Phone Numb	Website User Name	Website Password	Bill Day	Due Day
3	Wise Owl Wireless	1111111111111111	(800) 555-5555	UserName	GYHoots$24S7	4	28

Medical Bills and Miscellaneous Debts

When opening your medical bills and other miscellaneous debts, you will often find multiple copies of the same bill. Find the oldest and newest copies of each bill and throw away the rest. Use the Debt sheet to enter the service date (the date the bill was incurred) into the Service Date column of the table. You need to enter identifying details of the debt, as well as the amount owed, into the Debt Info sheet.

	A	B	C	D	E	F
1	**Debt Information**					
2	Debt	Account #	Customer/Patient /Client	Phone Number	Date of Service	Amount Owed
3	Community Hospital	18399209-02	Jackie	733-243-2918	2/23/2016	$725.00
4	Emergency Physicians Group	14387-1	Jackie	733-225-9045	2/23/2016	$435.00
5	Community Hospital	18357884-01	John	733-243-2918	4/6/2015	$84.00
6	Atlas Exterminators	34502	N/A	733-123-7654	5/14/2016	$75.00

Scan a copy of the bill into the correct folder and give it a name that will easily identify it.

:) › Bills › Medical

Name	^	Date modified
📄 Comm Hospital 18399209-02 Jackie 2-23-...		10/9/2016 1:00 PM

The Stuff You Forgot About

Earlier, I mentioned how when times were tight, I would watch in horror as little bills I had forgotten about, or didn't know when they were due, would post in my bank account and drop my balance below zero. I no longer have this problem because I have identified EVERY single recurring expense and eliminated many of them. Some of your recurring expenses won't be obvious until you have multiple months of transactions downloaded to your finance software. In the meantime, you can identify the amounts and posting dates of the expenses you do know about. Open your bank statements or print them out from online. Look for things you know are monthly expenses like Life Insurance, Bank Fees, Phone Insurance, Netflix and other online services. Each time you identify one, enter the information into the Recurring Expenses tab of the spreadsheet. Later, you will identify more, but it is important to get your head out of the sand when it comes to these little bills that add up. There is nothing quite like having a $6.99 phone insurance bill cost an additional $35 because you forgot it was due.

Think hard about expenses that come at other than monthly intervals. An example would be twice a year vehicle property taxes, yearly registration fees on multiple cars, professional fees, uniform expenses, service calls by exterminators and quarterly estimated taxes. Dig into your records, mail and bank statements to locate as many of these as you can find and then put them into the spreadsheet.

If you are self-employed or running a small business that is funded by you; come up with a monthly expense (or investment) amount that you can add to the spreadsheet as a single line item. You can use other spreadsheets or financial software to further itemize your business expenses. At this point, we are only concerned with how the business expenses effect the personal budget.

What's Next?

If we stopped here, you have enough information to make real changes to your financial condition and set up a decent budget. Don't overlook the section on recurring expenses. When most people make a budget, it is easy for them to list their rent, groceries and utilities. It is the small stuff like subscriptions, fees, Amazon Prime, phone insurance and the like that they forget about. These small recurring expenses can add up to hundreds of dollars that aren't in your budget.

Action Steps
Identify Your Expenses

Open your mail and identify all active accounts. Start looking at each entry in your bank statement that is not a purchase. Try to identify the purpose of each transaction. This is also a good time to look for possible fraudulent transactions. Then list three expenses that you forgot about. This could be a membership in some work-related organization or maybe a trial offer that you forgot about and are being billed for. It may also be a bill that you thought you had paid.

1. _____

2. _____

3. _____

Classify Your Expenses

After you have identified each expense, try to classify it. Is it a utility payment or a bill from the exterminator? Be specific, is it dining out or groceries? Is it a one time or recurring expense? For now, just write the classification right on the statement or printout. List two transactions that occur often enough they should be part of your budget.

1. _____

2. _____

Justify Your Expenses

After you have identified and classified each expense, try to justify it. Is it necessary? Could it be avoided? Is it a duplicate service? List two transactions that you could not justify.

1. _____

2. _____

Modify Your Unjustified Spending

If you are not able to justify an expense, you must modify or eliminate it. List three recurring expenses that need to be eliminated.

1. _____

2. _____

3. _____

Even if an expense is justified, it may need to be modified. List three recurring expenses that need to be modified. For instance, can you save money on a monthly payment by paying yearly? Would changing the method of payment save money?

1. _____

2. _____

3. _____

Chapter 4
Budget Basics

Zero-Based Budgeting

Zero-based budgeting works on the concept of having no unaccounted-for money at the end of the month. You must assign a purpose to every dollar. If you have $300 left over, you would assign it to savings or paying off a bill. When used with the concepts I've introduced in this book, zero-based budgeting will provide a framework in which to take control of your finances.

Zero-based budgeting will only work if you stay within the boundaries you set each month. At the end of each month, you are supposed to analyze your spending and adjust where your money goes. This will work for people who have much more income than expenses. If you are like I was, with no surplus money at the end of the month, you need to do more than just shuffle your money around from one category to another. You need to reduce your spending, increase your income, or both.

Many of my readers will find that working with a basic Zero-based budget, if they have decreased their expenses, will provide enough improvement in their financial situation that they won't need to do anything else. That is fine. Get with your mentor and set up your budget if you haven't done so already. I truly believe that while a zero-based budget will work for many people, it will not work by itself unless you know, *on a daily basis*, your balances and pending expenses. Your budget will not work if you only look at it once a month.

I want to remind my readers that I read numerous budgeting books and tried to use the budget ideas I found. I had limited success because of several factors. I had a variable income that I thought was hard to predict. I was almost always a month behind on all monthly bills like Electricity and Mortgage. I also had no discipline over my discretionary spending. The biggest problem I found with budgets was that they weren't very flexible, or they weren't interactive. Some of the budgets I have worked with were so complex that only a Certified Public Accountant could make sense of them. I knew what was happening with my money and could even predict when there would be problems, but I was helpless to prevent those problems because I had not clamped down on the undisciplined spending and never built up a buffer.

When I finally understood the underlying principles of Zero-based budgeting, I was able to combine the philosophy of Zero-based budgeting with self-discipline, tracking and analysis to produce results that are nothing short of phenomenal. I was facing financial disaster, so I spent about one month analyzing my finances and eliminating all undisciplined spending. With the help of a mentor, I confirmed that I was on the right track. I followed the steps introduced in the previous chapters. **I started assigning a purpose to each dollar**. I asked for and received additional hours at my job, which introduced more cash into the equation.

Three months later I was completely caught up on all my bills and had made five mortgage payments in three months. You would not believe how good it felt to look at my computer and see zeros on the balances of all my utility accounts. In month three, every single one of my bills was missing the familiar past due amount. I can't guarantee that you will turn your situation around as quickly as I did, because I don't know how much time and effort you will devote to your finances and I don't know how deeply underwater you are swimming. I can guarantee that if you follow the guidelines in this book, you will see an improvement in your situation.

I would like to share some more thoughts on assigning a purpose to every dollar. A zero-based budget does not mean that your balance is zero. It means that every dollar accomplishes something. That purpose might be to pay a bill. It might be to add padding to a minimum balance in an account. It might be to make a purchase you have been delaying until you can pay cash for it. If your goal is to have a minimum balance of $1000 in your checking account, then every dollar above that should have a different purpose.

Treat Your Household Like a Business

I was only able to make Zero based budgeting work when I treated my household as if it were a business. The business version of zero-based budgeting is much stricter than the household version. Every activity and every recurring expense are examined. If a recurring expense is not justifiable, it is eliminated or modified. If you recall, the second chapter of this book showed ways to eliminate unnecessary spending.

Standard Zero-based budgeting does not eliminate unnecessary spending. It just places it into a box and gives it a nice sounding name. This is fine if you already have more income than expenses. However, if you are constantly having financial difficulty, more drastic measures need to be taken. It is not enough to make an educated guess about what your expenses and income will be. Once a month analysis is not enough. You need to spend time on your finances EVERY SINGLE DAY. You need to analyze EVERY SINGLE EXPENSE. You also need to assign a purpose to EVERY SINGLE dollar.

Are You a Card Person or a Cash Person?

Many budget systems use an envelope system to help put a wall between you and your money. The idea is that if the money is in an envelope instead of your bank account, you will have less of a chance to spend the money meant for bills. I agree that it is very important to separate your daily spending from your bills and recurring expenses. Your expense account must be untouched by random spending. Most of these budget systems recommend putting your debit cards in a drawer and only using them for online payments of bills. We will be using envelopes, but in a modified fashion that will depend upon what type of income you and your spouse receive and if you are a cash person or card person. Very often one spouse will be a cash person and the other spouse a dedicated card person.

So, what is the difference between the two types of people? A cash person likes to have money in his pocket or her purse, but it doesn't stay there for long. If you hand them 20 one-dollar bills in the morning, they will have a pocket or purse full of change at the end of the day. Hand that same amount of money to a card person and you will find the money stashed in a secret fold of their wallet or purse.

The opposite holds true if you give each of them a debit card. A card person might make five to ten purchases a day on the card, while a cash person might make several purchases, all of which he reluctantly uses the card for because he ran out of cash. A major aspect of gaining control of your finances is fiscal accountability. If you oversee the family finances, you must have someone, either your spouse or mentor, hold you accountable. One reason for needing the accountability is that people who have habit and addiction spending become adept at hiding their expenses. I call them Cash-oholics and Card-oholics.

Cash-oholics

A cash person will often make ATM withdrawals instead of using a card because they like using cash better. However, there is a type of cash person I refer to as a *cash-oholic*. Cash-oholics prefer using cash because it allows them to hide spending on things that would be embarrassing if they showed up on a bank statement or receipt. The cash could be used for something as innocuous as sneaking off to see a movie but is often used to cover addiction purchases. A way to spot a cash-oholic is to look for frequent or large cash withdrawals from the bank. It is not uncommon to see $100 withdrawals with no explanation.

If you are a cash-oholic and have used cash in the past to cover your activities, it is time to end those behaviors. Once again, I will not spend time discussing the moral implications of various behaviors. Instead, let's look at the undocumented expenses that have been leaking from your cash basket. There is no way for you to justify withdrawing $100 cash to spend on an addiction. Own up to the addiction and start documenting it in your finances.

My suggestion if you are a cash person or a cash-oholic is to use your debit card, but only if you are tracking your expenses daily. If you decide to use cash for your purchases, keep the cash in an envelope, not in your pocket. Keep receipts for all your purchases and talk to your spouse and mentor if you are having problems with undisciplined or addiction spending.

Card-oholics

A card-oholic uses a debit or credit card to pay for addictive and habit spending. These purchases are often "guilty pleasures" like visiting the nail salon, purchasing chocolate or buying a lottery ticket. Combining a card-oholic and shopaholic in the same person is a financial train wreck waiting to happen. If you need to shop, visit the salon, browse the tool section at the Hardware Store or get your hair done as a coping mechanism for the stress in your life, make it a spending category and designate some money for it.

A card-oholic who is trying to hide morally questionable purchases from his or her spouse will often buy a pre-paid credit card or open a bank account in a different bank without telling anyone. My wife reminded me that sometimes a spouse will get a pre-paid card, so they can hide a gift they want to surprise their spouse with or they might have received one as a gift, so don't jump to conclusions if you find your spouse has a pre-paid card.

If you or your spouse is a card person or card-oholic, it is truly important for you to use the envelope system until you develop enough discipline to stop all unbudgeted spending. Make sure to keep the receipts and put them into the proper envelopes until you can photograph or scan the receipts. Every receipt needs to be recorded. It is impossible to be accountable with your finances if you have untracked spending.

Envelope Accounting and Accountability

Whether you ultimately decide to stick with a budget or move on to tracking, control and forecasting, you will need to use envelopes for any cash-based spending. Most of our parents or grandparents used some form of envelope system for their cash. If they were smart, they kept track of their spending right on the envelope. This is where I believe many people have failed to properly use the envelope system. They put their money in an envelope and they even remember the admonition that once the money is spent, there will be no more. Unfortunately, they can't remember where all the money went once the envelope is empty. This is a sign of laziness and unaccountability. The envelope system will only work properly if you track each expense.

It is very difficult to be accountable and keep accurate records without saving cash receipts and writing down the amounts. Mike, a friend of mine from Church, noted that people have difficulty doing 3rd grade math when it comes to family finances. It is simple arithmetic-adding and subtracting. This arithmetic should be completed right on the envelope. Enter the initial amount of cash and then write down each transaction amount, date and purpose.

Later, when you are using finance software, you can enter these transactions into your Petty Cash or envelope account. This is extremely important if you are using cash from envelopes to pay for business expenses such as meetings or travel expenses. Here is an example of how to track spending on an envelope.

Notice that in the above example, the numbers are rounded to the nearest dollar. Do not try to track your cash purchases to the penny. Instead, put your change into a change bucket in your car, or a jar (or piggy bank) at home. The change will start adding up and can be used for those times you feel the need to spend unbudgeted money.

I suggest that you keep the receipts in the envelope until you can record the purchases. If you can take a picture of each receipt, it will not be necessary to keep them. If your envelope gets covered in math and you still have money left, get a new envelope and start over. Make sure to enter the transactions in your finance software or expense tracker.

Card-based Envelope Accounting

There are some situations in which envelopes with cash are not a good idea. If you are in a situation where someone could pilfer from the envelopes or if you or your spouse has little or no control over their spending when there is cash available, then you should consider using a debit card from a dedicated allowance account. I only advise this if you are keeping frequent (daily or close to daily) track of your purchases. It is extremely important to keep your discretionary purchases separate from your recurring expenses. You must have a limit on your discretionary spending. If you allocate $200 each week for allowance, then you must stick to this amount.

The problem with using an allowance account instead of envelopes is that it is much easier to pull out the card for multiple purchases than to pull the money out of an envelope. However, both systems rely on the person using them having a degree of self-discipline. If you are not able to control your spending and be accountable to yourself, then you should find someone to be accountable to.

Accountability-Based Finances

It is very important to be accountable to someone in your finances, especially if you are a card-oholic or cash-oholic. This can be your spouse or your mentor, but they need to be familiar with accounting principles or have experience working with budgets. Don't run out and hire an accountant unless you have such a complicated financial situation that you need an accountant to straighten it all out. While accountants are important for business finance and for people with multi-million-dollar incomes, all an accountant can do is help you to track your finances and assist you with your taxes.

You need someone to hold you to account until you have learned to be completely honest with yourself. You need to print your Financial Picture spreadsheet and review it with your spouse and then have your mentor or someone else you trust, look at it. You don't need a high-priced financial planner or an accountant for this. Chances are, your mentor won't be a financial guru, but he will be successful in his field and have gained control of his own finances. He will see your blind spots and help you keep your goals in sight.

Pros and Cons of Budgets

I mentioned earlier that I found most budget plans to either be too simplistic, not matching my situation; or too complex, needing excessive amounts of time to fill in, modify and keep up with. I will not be teaching you how

68

to do a complex budget. I will explain how to set up a basic budget because it is necessary for setting a framework and for explaining your finances to a mentor or lender.

The problem with most budgets is that they don't address the issues of undisciplined spending and controlling exactly when and where your money is spent. Just as an example, the standard budget will have a space for utilities. But you might have Electricity, Natural Gas, Sewage and Water. None of these utilities are going to cost the same each month. They depend on usage, which can vary depending on the season and other factors.

The varying costs of most utilities are one reason why my recurring expense sheet has a column for each month. By putting in the monthly amounts for each utility over the previous year, you can make an accurate guess as to what the future costs will be. A normal budget will only take the average of these costs unless you change the figure every month. Using the budget form introduced earlier, you can take the average cost shown in the last column of the recurring expense sheet and enter that into the budget form.

Your basic budget should be based on categories, not individual expenses. For example, instead of having five separate entries for five utilities, add up the average amounts shown in the recurring expense sheet and make one entry for utilities. The basic budget is mainly for reference use. It is not meant as a tool for financial control, it is more of an overview. If you only use a budget, whether basic or complex, and don't plot out your recurring expenses, you will quickly run into problems.

Another problem with most budgets is that the ones that are detailed enough to provide control over your finances are very time intensive. You must constantly adjust them to match current income and spending and you often must save and start over each month in a new tab or spreadsheet. Standard budget forms usually don't work well with variable incomes and expenses. They assume that everything will continue as it has in the past and don't account for unexpected changes in income and expenses. This is the reason I recommend using some form of finance software such as Quicken or Mint.

Finance software usually involves a learning curve and setup time but is much less time intensive than spreadsheet budgets. After seeing some of the problems with budgets, you might be asking yourself, "Why should I have a budget?" A basic budget is a useful starting point and is helpful as an overview of your finances. A basic budget is also useful for showing how much income is expected to come in and what expenses are expected to come out during each month.

Even if you use finance software, a spreadsheet budget is necessary when some expenses and directing of money is based on percentages. Some examples that rely on percentages are tithing and charity giving, savings and debt reduction. Most finance software is not set up to calculate percentages. If you are planning on giving percentages of your income to charity, savings and debt reduction, then a spreadsheet budget can easily calculate those numbers for you. This is especially important with variable incomes.

There should be money left over after the recurring expenses are accounted for. Using zero based budgeting principles, the left-over money should be assigned a purpose. The question then is, to what purpose should the money be assigned. Many people will suggest putting it into savings or debt reduction. This is fine, if you have a cushion built up. The reason that most people run into financial difficulties is that they have not built themselves a cushion. They are treading water, and every wave that comes along is a potential crisis. Your budget should now reflect the recurring expenses you have identified and should show a positive balance due to the money you have freed up that used to go towards undisciplined and untracked spending.

More Reasons Why a Budget is Necessary

While I have stated that a budget by itself isn't enough for controlling your finances, it plays a necessary role. When most people think of a budget, they picture a set of boundaries that limit their spending. A budget is a category-based spending proposal. It is almost impossible to track individual purchases using a budget, but a budget is an important tool for deciding what categories you will spend your money on. Without a budget, tracking your purchases will serve no purpose. The budget is what defines your spending plan. Tracking, identifying, justifying and modifying expenses is what allows you to keep within the boundaries set by the budget. Without at least a basic budget, you will be guessing at how much you can afford to allocate to each spending category. On the other hand, without the effort of tracking your finances, your budget is a worthless piece of guesswork.

I would like to remind my readers that I spent years of tracking my finances until I stopped because I was discouraged at the lack of results. It wasn't until I made a basic budget and used it as a framework for my tracking that I was able to gain full control of my finances. I had tried numerous budget plans and ideas, but they never worked for me until I used them in coordination with my detailed tracking on finance software.

A basic budget is necessary because it provides a necessary framework for financial planning. A zero-based budget is necessary because it provides the framework for directing the left-over money. Neither type of budget will work for you if you don't constantly adjust them to reflect reality.

Why a Budget Can't Stand Alone

A major flaw of budgets is that they assume that expenses and income will continue as they always have before. A budget assumes that a person's paycheck will be the same, week after week. A budget doesn't make allowance for variable income or bills. Software such as Quicken does have budgeting that allows you to put in different amounts for each category every month. While this seems helpful, I have found that in real-life applications, it becomes very time-intensive and next to useless. My best success has come from using a spreadsheet based, basic budget as a framework for allocating funds in combination with finance software. I spend about ten minutes every month on my budget and about 5 minutes every day on daily tracking using my finance software.

If you haven't already downloaded the budget sheet from my website www.gyhootsbook.com, do so now. It is free. It is simple. It will provide the foundation you need to take full control of your finances. If you have a budget book or spreadsheet that you like, then update it using the recurring expense information I talked about earlier. Go back and read Chapter Three and put together a basic budget. Don't worry about perfection at this point. You are building a framework and can adjust the budget later. Right now, it is important that you know all your recurring expenses and put them into categories. Should you have a budget? Most definitely. A budget is simply a statement of how much income you expect and how you plan to spend it. My point is that you must have a budget to succeed, but a budget is not enough. It is a starting point.

Budget Review

In Chapter Three we talked about how to gather all the information needed to set up a temporary budget. Now let's apply what we've learned and done since and setup a Monthly Budget. If you look closely at the temporary budget on the next page, you will notice that there are no entries for savings or asset building. The monthly budget will have an entry for savings. There are several entries that appear at first glance to be used for debt reduction but, they are only minimum payments. Debt reduction only counts when you pay extra.

Notice that the temporary budget shows that Bob and Sally freed up $500 on paper, which is almost 10%. Most people who don't control their finances will waste that money. In Chapter Six, we will talk about various strategies for debt reduction and savings. For now, and in the next chapter, we will focus on clearing up 20% of your income and using it to quickly build a $1000 Emergency Fund and then a cushion of at least one month of expenses. In our example, Bob and Sally need to find a way to trim an additional $700 from their budget to reach the target of $1200 (20 percent).

Notice that they had $800 per month going towards miscellaneous expenses. When they researched their spending, they found that $380 of the total was for things that they could classify and justify. These became recurring expenses. An example was $40 each month in toll road payments so that Bob could get to work. The other $420 was being wasted on habit and impulse buying. They called their insurance company and saved $80 and have now freed up 20% of their income.

Temporary Budget

Net Income	Monthly	Weekly
Bob Salary	$4,200	$1,050
Sally Paycheck	$600	$150
Sally Tip Income	$1,200	$300
Total Net Income	$6,000	$1,500

Expenses	Monthly	Weekly
Tithes	$600	$150
Mortgage or Rent	$1,300	$325
Groceries	$500	$125
Household	$200	$50
Electricity	$300	$75
Water	$100	$25
Natural Gas	$150	$38
Internet/Cable	$120	$30
Cell Phone	$150	$38
Car payment	$300	$75
Car Insurance	$220	$55
Gas	$240	$60
Bob Allowance	$200	$50
Sally Allowance	$300	$75
Credit Card Payments	$300	$75
Medical Bills	$100	$25
Student Loan Payments	$220	$55
Miscellaneous	$800	$200
Total Expenses	$5,500	$1,375

	Monthly	Weekly
Target Amount (20%)	$1,200	$300
Freed Up Money	$500	$125

Now let's look at the monthly budget Bob and Sally set up after cutting out all unnecessary spending.

Monthly Budget

Net Income	Monthly	Weekly
Bob Salary	$4,200	$1,050
Sally Paycheck	$600	$150
Sally Tip Income	$1,200	$300
Total Net Income	**$6,000**	**$1,500**
Expenses	**Monthly**	**Weekly**
Tithes	$600	$150
Mortgage or Rent	$1,300	$325
Groceries	$500	$125
Household	$200	$50
Utilities	$820	$205
Recurring Expenses	$380	$95
Car payments	$300	$75
Car Insurance	$140	$35
Bob Allowance	$300	$75
Sally Allowance	$340	$85
Debt/Savings Etc.		
Credit Card Payments	$200	$50
Medical Bills	$100	$25
Student Loan Payments	$220	$55
Debt Reduction		$0
Savings		$0
Asset Building		$0
Total Expenses	**$4,800**	**$1,200**
Target Amount (20%)	$1,200	$300
Difference	**$1,200**	**$300**

Notice that the debt reduction, savings and asset-building sections are empty. How you fill those in will be determined by your individual situation and the advice of your mentor. If you are behind on all your utilities, you need to use the money you freed up to get caught up and ahead on your payments. Then you should to set aside $1000 for the emergency fund.

Bob and Sally added some of their habit spending to their personal allowance so that things like the morning cup of coffee become a budget item. By trimming the fat off their spending, they now have choices. They can build up their savings and start paying off debt. They can also invest into building an asset.

Think about the reality of what you see in those two budgets. Bob and Sally were wasting $1200 each month that is now going to allow them to build up a cash reserve and pay off their debts in a very short period. They will have freed up $14,400 over the next year. Your situation might be different. Let's suppose that you are making $3,000 per month. If you free up 20% of your income, that is $600 per month or $7200 over the next year. The timeframes shown in the next chapter will still hold true as long as you have been keeping your bills in line with your income.

Before you decide what to do with your freed-up money, read the following chapters on building a breakwater and tracking your finances. The budget you have or will set up is a physical statement of your good intentions. To make your intentions a reality, you have to track your spending and make course corrections and adjustments.

Action Steps

1. Take your temporary budget and make the necessary adjustments to turn it into a monthly budget.

2. If you haven't reached your target percentage of freed up money, go back and see if anything else can be modified or eliminated.

3. Buy a box of plain envelopes and set up your envelope system.

4. Start using the envelopes to keep and track the cash that you use for purchases.

5. Decide if you are a cash person or a card person and adjust your plan of action to take this into account.

6. Be honest with yourself and decide if you are a cash-o-holic or card-o-holic.

7. If you are using secret accounts or cards to hide destructive behavior or extremely wasteful habits, seek help or counseling.

Chapter 5
Building a Breakwater

In Chapter One, we discussed initial steps to start building a cushion or a breakwater against the storms. Two of those steps are to create a $1000 emergency fund and to work towards paying your bills when they are posted, not when they are due. The purpose of these two steps is to create a buffer for unexpected emergencies. By paying your bills when they are posted, you create a buffer of about 45 days. Let's say that your car fails inspection and the repair is beyond your mechanical ability. You are told that it will cost $1200 to fix the problems. If you have an emergency fund in place, you can use part or all of it, and then shift the payment of one of your bills to a later date. Since you were originally planning on paying it when posted, you can hold off paying the bill for several weeks before it is due.

As you start freeing up money by eliminating unnecessary spending, you should simultaneously add money to your emergency fund and bring all your monthly bills (rent, electricity, credit card, etc.) current. If you are presently behind on many of your bills, this process will take about two months to complete. It is a matter of discipline and should be the highest priority you have in your finances. If you have unpaid bills such as medical co-payments or any other debt that is not a recurring expense, they should be entered into the debt sheet.

Call each creditor and explain that you would like to start payment arrangement after you have caught up on your monthly bills. When you explain that you should be able to start within the next two months, most of them will be happy to set up an arrangement with you. It is important to first get your monthly bills caught up and build the $1000 emergency fund. Once you have the emergency fund built up, it may be worthwhile considering putting it into a Certificate of Deposit (CD). Most CDs will pay a better interest rate and are available for immediate withdrawal. Banks and Credit Unions usually allow 2-5 free withdrawals per year. I found out that keeping my emergency fund in a normal savings account didn't work well because it was difficult to keep it separate from my normal finances. A CD solves the problem.

The process of building a breakwater is multistepped. It starts small, with the $1000 emergency fund and ends large with a reserve of six months of income. How long this takes will depend on your income and the amount of money you have freed up. In this example, we will assume that Bob and Sally have $6000 of Net Income per month and have freed up 20 percent ($1200). Here is what the process looks like if they apply the entire 20% toward savings:

$1000 Emergency Fund	**1 Month**
Bills Caught Up	**1-3 Months**
1 Month of Expenses in Bank	**3-4 Months**
1 Month of Income in Bank	**5-6 Months**

Once they have one month of income in the bank, Bob and Sally should start applying about half of their freed-up money toward debt reduction. The scenarios can get really complicated depending on how much debt reduction is needed, so we will assume in this illustration that there is no debt. Bob and Sally are applying 20% of their income towards building a cushion.

3 Months Expenses in Bank	**9 Months**
3 Months Income in Bank	**14 Months**
6 Months Expenses in Bank	**18 Months**
6 Months Income in Bank	**28 Months**

Earlier, I strongly advised finding a mentor or coach. When you have brought your monthly bills current and have the $1000 emergency fund in place, it is time to sit down with your mentor and decide how to apportion the freed-up funds. The above numbers are for illustration purposes only. Everyone has a unique situation and only you and your mentor can determine the correct way to disburse your funds. Your mentor may suggest various combinations of savings, debt reduction and business investment. If, however, your mentor suggests investing into a proven business opportunity that will create an asset or cash flow, while at the same time directing the remainder of the money to reducing your debt and building up your savings, then you are getting good advice. A good guideline would be to limit yourself or the person you are mentoring to investing ten percent of the net income into any business or investment.

Use Bank Accounts as a Breakwater

One of the reasons that various financial advisors suggest the use of envelopes is that it keeps your spending away from your bank account. As we discussed earlier, this is effective only if you track your transactions on the envelopes and then transfer those transactions to financial software. I can't emphasize enough how important it is to use financial software of some sort. It is also important to keep your money in one location until you have more money than can be insured by the FDIC. I would recommend using a Credit Union if you have access to one.

If you decide that it would be convenient to change banks, then move all your accounts there (unless of course you are a millionaire). Why is this so important? You need the ability to move money from one account to another. This becomes critical as you start to manipulate your accounts to pay bills and build up the breakwater. It is also important to have more than one account. I currently have four checking accounts and five savings accounts in the same Credit Union. You may only need three checking and savings accounts if you own your own business, but you might need four, if you are going to use your debit card instead of envelopes. At a minimum, you need two checking and two savings accounts (Normally each checking account is linked to a savings account).

There are many ways to determine where your funds will go and to which accounts. I will try to make it as simple as possible for you. When I first heard this concept, I had two bank accounts (each with attached savings) but was not effectively distributing my money. At a minimum, you need an Operating Account and an Expense Account. If you own a small business, you need an account for the business. Check with your mentor if this should be an actual business (DBA) account, or just a normal account you use to conduct your business with. If you plan to use a debit card instead of cash for daily transactions, you need to open a Spending Account. Each of these accounts need to be set up so they are connected to and can draw from each other.

Operations Checking Account

The Operations Checking account is where all your deposits should go. This is the clearing house account. All your funds will be distributed from here. Eventually, you should have a minimum of one month of income sitting in this account after you have a month of expenses in the Expense Checking account. Until then, try to maintain at least $100 in this account. The debit card for this account should be stored in a safe place and not be routinely used for anything.

Operations Savings Account

This account should be used for general savings and an emergency fund. Exercise extreme discipline with this account. No matter how tight your situation is, you need to put money into this account on a regular basis. This account is the foundation of your break wall. Eventually you may want to have 3-6 months of income sitting in this account. When you have reached that level, any additional savings should go into high-yield accounts. Check with your mentor about how many months of income you should have in this account.

Expense Checking Account

The Expense Checking Account is the account used to pay all scheduled expenses other than business and discretionary spending. Earlier we talked about getting one month of expenses in the bank. This is the first account that should hold that money. This is the account that needs to be watched daily. If you have a debit card for this account, use it for online bill paying, but do not use it for anything else.

Expense Savings Account

This account should be used for holding the money that you set aside each payday for larger bills such as rent or mortgage. Keep the money in this account until needed to pay the large bill. This allows you to see at a glance if you have the money set aside for the large expense. Don't use this for ordinary monthly bills, as many banks will charge fees for excessive withdrawals from a savings account.

Spending Checking Account

This is the account that you use for discretionary spending, allowance, date nights, etc. Until you have built up several months of income in the other accounts, you should track this account closely. Only put in enough money to cover the budget for these items. If you need to buy something that is not part of the budget, you need to check with your spouse or mentor because it is probably an impulse buy. If the purchase is justified, then transfer the money from the Operations Account. If there isn't enough money in the operations account, then you should probably hold off on the purchase.

This account can also be used for budget items like groceries and clothing that may involve multiple purchases. You would still only put enough money in the account to cover the budget for these categories, but this way, you are not endangering your ability to pay your bills because you spent too much on groceries.

When you have reached your goal of having at least six months of income sitting in your Operations Savings account and you are debt-free, this is the account where you would put your fun money into. When you reach this level, you deserve to have some extra fun, if you make it a budget item.

Spending Savings Account

This account should be used for building a cushion for daily and discretionary spending. A good goal would be to have a week's worth, and then a month's worth of discretionary spending in the savings account. Don't focus on this account until after you have put your recurring expense cushion in place.

Business Checking Account

Whether this account needs to be a true business account, or a personal account used for business will depend on local laws and the type of business you own. It is safer, legally, to open a regular business account. This usually costs more and involves getting a business license and possible incorporation. As a rule of thumb, you don't need a regular business account if you use your own personal vehicle and don't need checks with the business name on them. If you are unsure, get your head out of the sand and find out. Call the local Chamber of Commerce or check with City Hall.

For small businesses, you will need to have this account attached to your personal accounts if you are funding the business strictly through your own efforts and money. Tax time is much easier if you pay all your business expenses using this account. Do not use this account for anything that is not tax deductible unless your business coach or mentor says otherwise.

Business Savings Account

Use the business savings account to build up funds for conventions, tools, advertising and other expenses that don't occur monthly.

Putting It All Together

Is your head spinning from all these different types of accounts? Don't worry. It will make sense to you once you've read through the account descriptions several times. Start by opening a second account (checking and savings together) if you don't have one already. If you already have direct deposit and automatic bill payments on the first account, you need to separate the income from the expenses. The easiest way to do this is to change your direct deposit to the new account. However, if you have multiple direct deposits from sources other than a job, then it may be easier to change your online payments to the new account.

The Expense Account is only used to pay recurring expenses. It should not be used for purchases of any kind. It should also not be used to withdraw cash for spending or allowance. Remember that funds are disbursed from the Operating Account, not the Expense Account. Once you have your expense and operating accounts set up and running smoothly, you should consider opening a Spending (Allowance) Account which you would use for budget items such as groceries, clothing and allowance.

Connecting the Accounts

Most banks and credit unions allow multiple accounts to be linked to each other. This makes it easier to transfer money between the accounts. You can also set up overdraft between accounts that don't need protection. This is helpful when you have a bill come in and forgot to transfer the money to cover it. Instead of charging a fee, the bank will automatically transfer the needed money from one account to the other. Here are my recommendations for linking accounts.

1. Operating Account checking and savings overdraft to Expense Account, Allowance Account and Business Account checking and savings.
2. Expense Account savings only overdrafts to Expense Account checking.
3. Expense Account checking overdrafts to Allowance Account checking.

Other Scenarios

Sometimes your situation doesn't fit into a nice box. An example of this would be if husband and wife have separate accounts from before they were married and choose to keep them separate. This may be needed in a case where one spouse may not be as accountable with money as the other. It may also be needed if the couple is filing taxes separately, such as when one spouse is part of a Limited Liability Company or Sole Proprietorship. The key here is communication and at least one shared expense account in which both contribute to pay for shared expenses like car payment and rent. The debit cards for this account should be used for shared online bill pay, but the cards issued to the account should be stored in a safe place and not used for daily purchases.

If you decide to take control of your finances, but your spouse or partner doesn't, you can still make a difference in your situation by doing your part. If your significant other keeps dipping into the savings account, you might want to consider opening an account that only you have access to, but with them as the beneficiary in case something happens to you. Don't do this in secret unless you are in a bad situation. Talk to your spouse and come to an agreement of how to change direction. Ask them to let you experiment and maybe they will agree to join you when they see the good results.

Everybody's situation is different. Learn to think outside the box. Learn the principles of financial accountability and then apply them to your unique situation.

Variable Income

A breakwater is critical for people who receive sporadic or variable income. By building up a reserve, the money will be available in the down times between jobs or paychecks. If you have a variable income, it is important for you to cut back on all unnecessary spending until you have your reserve in place. Generally, even with a variable income, it is possible to estimate the amount that will be received for the current job. Make sure to enter that estimate into your basic budget and the financial software.

If your income is variable in the amount you receive, you should treat each paycheck the same way you would a normal one. Disburse the necessary money to the Expense and Spending accounts and if you have money left over, put that money in the appropriate savings accounts.

If your income is variable in when you receive it, then disburse the funds based on when you expect your next check. If you receive three months income in one check, but don't know when you will receive the next one, then put three months' worth of money in each appropriate account. Act as if you won't get paid for four months. Don't forget to set aside the estimated taxes if applicable. Put the tax money into your Expense Savings Account unless you have another account for that purpose. If you have variable income, you are probably already doing some form of this. It is really important for people with variable income to build up the cash reserve.

Tip or Other Cash Income

If you receive tip income or cash payments for work, it is easy to waste the money. I solved this for myself by making envelopes for gas, groceries, allowance and other bills that I paid in cash. I also had an envelope for a weekly cash deposit into the Operating Account. Since I am a cash person, it was important to keep the transactions and receipts.

I would receive different amounts every day, but when I started tracking how much I received, I noticed that each day of the week produced similar results each week. I started estimating my tips in Quicken using the add income reminder option in the bills window. Suddenly, I could predict with great accuracy how much my variable tip income would be. Some days, I would count my tip money and find that I had made exactly what I had predicted. My tip income became a valuable resource that played a great role in allowing us to gain control of our finances.

Set aside the taxable portion of your tip income into the Expense Savings Account. Remember to make your tip income a budget item, not just pocket money. I would also recommend using the deposits from your tip money to build your cushion whenever possible. Your mentor may suggest using the tip money to pay for extra business expenses once you are caught up with all your bills. Think of tip money as cushion money. Don't make a critical bill payment dependent on money that you may or may not receive. Tip money is a resource that will speed up the process of building a cushion.

Scheduling Payments

One of the reasons for building a break water is to smooth out the waves. When your account balances are graphed they should look nice and smooth. If they look like a storm, then your finances probably feel like a storm. Much of this can be avoided by rescheduling payments to match income dates. If you are caught up on your bills, then it makes more sense to pay a large bill the day after you get paid instead of the day before. The recurring expense sheet should have the due dates of each bill. Plan appropriately.

Any boater can tell you that the deeper the water, the smoother the waves. You can ride the waves if you have some water under you. Your goal is to smooth out the waves by actively coordinating your bill due dates with your income. Move the bills around so that you never have major ups and downs in your account balances. Develop a cushion that will help you deal with rogue waves.

It is important to not spend all your money before your next paycheck, even if you are behind. No matter what, always have something in the bank. If you have a bill that must be paid but paying it will bring you down to a dangerous bank balance, then call the company and explain the situation. See if you can hold off on paying the bill till your next paycheck and do your best to catch up on the rest of the payments. It is critical to put money into savings each payday. If you cut out all unnecessary spending, you should be able to save and catch up on all your bills. If you can't, then you need to increase your income or start cutting out non-essentials like Cable, Software and anything else you are spending money on that is not critical.

Your ability to self-schedule payments without being penalized with late fees is dependent on whether you have built up a cushion in your expense account. When you have a cushion built up, you have greater flexibility. Normally you would want to schedule the payment during the period between when it is billed and when it is due, but after the nearest pay day. If you are still building up a cushion, you will probably be scheduling it after the due date, but before it becomes past due (because the next bill came out). If you are still building your cushion, then try to schedule the payment immediately after the pertinent pay day. Remember: the goal is to pay all recurring expenses when they are billed, not when they are due.

Automatic Payments

If you are still in the process of building a cushion for your finances, you need to consider temporarily cancelling automatic payments and online bill pay. These payment alternatives offer the ability to have your payments come out of your bank account automatically. This is fine if you have built up a good cushion, but they are inflexible. They can cause problems when you are trying to smooth out and fix your finances because the institutions don't care what your bank balance is, they just know that there is supposed to be enough to pay their bill.

It's all well and good to have your phone bill automatically withdrawn from your bank account. But, if you get paid on the first of the month and the bill is being paid on the 30th, it can cause some problems. I would recommend only keeping automatic bill pay with those bills that offer substantial discounts for doing so. As an example, as soon as I built up a cushion, I set up automatic payments for my automobile insurance. I save about $300 per year by doing this. On the other hand, by paying my mortgage at the local branch, I save about $140 per year. This is because they charge $12 per online payment.

Many small recurring expenses are costing you money. An example is when you pay for software or some other service monthly instead of a yearly. You can save a lot of money by paying yearly instead of monthly. Once you have built up your cushion, look at each monthly expense and see if it can be converted to a yearly or quarterly expense.

Manual Payments

The main problem with making payments manually is that they can be time-consuming, and you can forget about them. If you are lazy, then you might just need to stick to automatic bill-pay. Then again, if you are lazy, nothing in this book is going to help you solve your problems. It will take time and self-discipline to gain control of your finances. Until you have a substantial reserve sitting in the bank, you need to take an extremely hands-on approach to bill payment. There should never be a week that you haven't updated your financial picture. There should never be a day when you don't know your bank balances. I can look at projected balances on Quicken and know exactly when every bill is going to be paid and what my bank balance will be, because every dollar has a purpose. Don't ever be surprised again. Know your balance. Pay your bills when you have them scheduled.

Mortgage Payment

I will not get into whether you should start making extra payments or paying off the mortgage early. That is between you and your financial counselor. Sometimes though, life happens, and you find yourself behind on your mortgage. It is very important to work with your mortgage lender to get caught up. Once you are caught up, I strongly advocate putting aside money for the mortgage payment into your savings account. As an example, if your mortgage payment is $1600 per month and you are paid weekly, you should put $400 into the Expense Savings Account after each paycheck. Divide each bill by the number of paychecks per month and designate that amount of money each paycheck.

Once you have caught up on all your bills and are paying them when they are billed, not when they are due; you should try to get into a position where you have the following month's mortgage payment on hand before the end of the month. Some mortgage lenders allow you to pay twice a month, if you are a month ahead on your payments. This has many benefits, including the ability to pay off the mortgage early. If disaster strikes, you are a month ahead.

Timely Payment

The main reason for paying all your bills as early as possible is that you build in an automatic cushion in case you have a loss of income or some other disaster. The other reason is just as important. If you pay after the due date, you have the stress of wondering if your Utilities are going to get cut off, your car repossessed, or if you'll get a visit from the Sheriff with an eviction notice or court summons.

Another less drastic reason for paying on time is that you avoid the continuous loss of money to late fees. My water company charges 10% of the bill if you are one day late. The Mortgage company charges $45 if you are 15 days late. Timely payment has the potential of saving you hundreds of dollars every year.

Peace of Mind

Suppose you were to be laid off or have an unexpected crisis. If you are behind on your bills and don't have a cushion built up, you will experience extreme anxiety and will worry about every single bill. Every time you or your spouse buys something, there will probably be an argument. Every bit of your focus and energy will revolve around money.

Now suppose that you are laid off or need a new transmission, but you have an Emergency Fund with $1000 and you have 3-6 months of expenses sitting in the bank. You might have to cancel your vacation, or put off buying a new car, but you have peace of mind because you know you have time and money to overcome the challenge.

Dreams

I believe everyone needs a dream. I'm not talking about a fantasy, but something you want to have or do that is currently not possible for you but is achievable if you continue to progress in your goals. It may be a house on the lake or a new car. It might be to become debt-free. Think about something that you want to have that will provide you an incentive to practice delayed gratification. Be specific. If it is a house, how many bedrooms, baths, etc. If it is a boat, how many engines, what model and what color. You might want to travel the world or go on missionary trips. Find a picture that matches your dream and put it somewhere like the bathroom mirror or the refrigerator, so you will see it every day. When you have tough times, remind yourself of what you are working towards.

I have heard many speakers tell how they had received exactly what they pictured. I had never personally experienced this until recently. Back in 1990, I test drove a Brand-New Jaguar 12-cylinder Convertible. I loved it and wanted it so bad I could taste it. It cost over $60,000 so I knew that I had a lot of hard work ahead of me before it would be sitting in my driveway. I hung a picture of the Jag on my refrigerator and it stayed there for many years. Eventually, after several moves, the picture was lost, and I only remembered my dream occasionally.

About five years ago, my daughter called and asked me if I could go to a nearby Foreign Car Repair Shop and buy a car for her with money she would send. It needed repair, so I had to tow it to my house. I worked on it for several years, but never got it running. However, for three years, every time I looked out into my driveway, I saw a 1990 twelve-cylinder Jaguar Convertible. I might have forgotten my dream, but apparently, God didn't. Sometimes, God does seem to have a sense of humor.

A dream only becomes a fantasy when you are not willing to do the work and delayed gratification necessary to obtain it. If you aren't sure if your dream is realistic, talk to someone who is where you want to be. Ask them if you are on the right track.

"DREAM BIG. THINK BIG. SPEND SMALL."

-LAWRENCE JACOB MAST

A long time ago, I realized that I would never achieve my dreams unless I first became financially sound. I tried to picture the dream of being debt free with money in the bank. I wrote a check to the Electric Company for an entire year of electricity. That original check is gone now, but I have written a new one and it is taped to the wall right behind my computer screen. I have a date written on that check and on that date, I will be taking the check off the wall. If the electric company accepts it, I will be paying a years' worth of electricity in one payment. I'll be doing the same with my other bills.

Find a way to express your dream of financial soundness. It may be a check to your church that equals a month of income. It could be a picture of a smashed alarm. It could be a picture of a new house or car. It may be as simple as a picture of a new suit cut from a magazine or a cruise you have put off for years. Put the picture or check on your refrigerator or someplace that you will see it every day. Whenever you get tired of practicing delayed gratification, look at the pictures and remember your dreams. Dreams do come true but making them happen is up to you.

Special Note to Network Marketers

If your business gives you a dream, let your business pay for the dream. Don't purchase a fancy car or $1000 Suit or Dress with the idea of impressing your prospects or downline unless it is appropriate for your level of business and your business provided the funds. What you do will be duplicated by your downline. If you are using your funds to imitate a level of success that you haven't legitimately reached, you risk having downline imitate you, which will mean financial disaster for some. You might have the funds available since you now have control of your finances, but the downline imitating you probably is living on the edge and your bad example could end up ruining their opportunity to succeed.

Goals

Goals are your hopes and dreams with dates attached to them. A dream without a date is a fantasy. If you can picture yourself living a stress-free life with no debt, no calls from collection agencies and thousands of dollars in the bank, that is a dream. Turn your dream into a goal. Write down what you want to have or accomplish and then set a date to it. Every time you walk away from an impulse purchase, you know that you are one step closer to making your dream a reality. Set short term and long-term goals. How much money do you want in your savings account in two months, two years, five years.

Action Steps

List the percentages of income you plan to use for the following categories:

1. Tithing _____

2. Savings _____

3. Debt Reduction _____

4. Asset Building _____

$1000 Emergency Fund _____

Bills Caught Up _____

1 Month of Expenses in Bank _____

1 Month of Income in Bank _____

3 Months Expenses in Bank _____

3 Months Income in Bank _____

6 Months Expenses in Bank _____

6 Months Income in Bank _____

GET YOUR HEAD OUT OF THE SAND

List five things you would like to have in the next five years that you could not do without gaining control of your finances. Put a date on them.

1._____ _____

2._____ _____

3._____ _____

4._____ _____

5._____ _____

List five things you would like to do in the next five years that you could not do without gaining control of your finances. Put a date on them.

1._____ _____

2._____ _____

3._____ _____

4._____ _____

5._____ _____

Chapter 6
Debt Reduction Strategies

There are almost as many strategies for reducing and eliminating debt as there are types of debt. You can get debt consolidation loans, take out a second mortgage, transfer your credit card balances to a new card or set aside a percentage of your income to pay off your debts. I recommend the last option in most cases. While there are always exceptions, it almost always makes more sense to pay off your debts with your freed-up income than any other option. Let's look at different types of debt and then develop a strategy for reducing and eliminating those debts. Always keep in mind that it is better to avoid debt in the first place than to have to pay it off.

Types of Debt

I am not going to try to talk about every type of debt. I will touch on some of the most common types of debt and then give some strategies for eliminating them. Your goal should be to eliminate all debt with the possible exception of your home.

Consumer Debt

Most Americans carry a high level of consumer debt. They owe money for credit cards, vehicles, boats, homes, school loans, personal loans, furniture, appliances, clothing, timeshares, etc. The one thing all consumer debt has in common is that the consumer made a choice to carry the debt instead of paying cash. Remember how we discussed delayed gratification? Start practicing delayed gratification now. Do not add any more consumer debt. Even when you have built your cushion and become debt-free, you should start paying cash or cash equivalent for consumer goods. Why would you want to add consumer debt when you worked so hard to become debt-free? The answer I have heard is that taking on debt helps raise your credit score. Your credit score only matters if you want to add more consumer debt. Smart people use that credit for building assets, not to buy cars, boats and luxury items. Build your credit by paying for a rental home, apartment complex or some other income producing property. If you want to borrow money from the bank to purchase a property that will produce substantial income, they will be more interested in your minimal debt load and money on hand than how many cars and televisions you are paying off and how many credit cards are in your wallet.

Educational Debt

School loans are a dead weight hanging around the necks of an entire generation of students. Let's compare two students. John went to a good State University, stayed in the dorms and payed about $20,000 per year for Tuition, Room and Board, Books and various classroom fees. His parents payed $20,000 and he received grants and scholarships worth another $20,000 and educational loans for the remaining $40,000. If he pays $400 per month it will take him over ten years to pay off this loan.

Bob went to a Community College for two years, received $2000 in Pell Grants, his parents paid $2000, he paid $2000 and he received a student loan for $2000 to get an Associate Degree. He got a decent paying job and then began taking night school to finish his bachelor's degree. Since he was living at home, he avoided room and board. Of the $20,000 required to finish his degree, he was able to get grants of $5000 and was able to pay $7000 from his job income. He received an educational loan for the remaining $8000. His total student loan debt is $10,000. Because of his work history, he is promoted after he gets his degree and can make payments of $500 per month. He pays off his loan in two years and is debt free. He just paid cash for his car ($10,000 used) and took his honeymoon in Europe (and paid cash for it).

John is still looking for the perfect job but is happy that manager at the computer store is letting him work overtime. He gets regular calls demanding payment on his student loan. He doesn't park his car in his driveway, because he is afraid it is going to get repossessed. Need I say more about educational loans?

Home Mortgage

As of this writing, the tax advantage for owning a home is on the brink of disappearing. If you are trying to decide whether to buy a home or not, don't make the decision based on a tax deduction that might be going away. If you have a mortgage, make sure you pay it in a timely manner. Don't try to pay off your mortgage early until you have full control of your finances and have become free of all other debt. If you are going to get a mortgage on a house, put down as large a down payment as you can afford. Once you have your mortgage, make it a high priority and try to have next month's payment sitting in the savings account this month.

Second Mortgage

I am talking about second mortgages separately from home mortgages because they are completely different in the reasons people get them. Most people who take out a second mortgage use the money for education, remodeling and debt consolidation. I consider each of these a dubious reason for putting your home at risk. Other reasons people give for taking out a second mortgage are even more dubious. Bail Bonds, vacations, luxury purchases, betting, investments and business startups.

Recently there have been reports of consumers who have taken out a second mortgage in order invest in cryptocurrency. This is a dangerous trend. Most of us would scorn a person who takes a second mortgage to play the lottery, gamble or invest in the stock market. The same scorn should be applied to people who take out a second mortgage for investment in an acknowledged bubble. The most famous example in recent history of the same magnitude of the current trend was the Tulip Mania of the 1600s. People invested money they had and money they didn't have into tulips. There were people who made their fortunes because they got in and out quickly. Most investors lost everything they owned when the tulip market crashed. People still remember this four hundred years later.

Investments that carry anything other than mild risk should be made only from money that is otherwise collecting dust in a bank account. The money should not be part of your six-month emergency fund. If you don't have six months of expenses sitting in the bank, then you are not prepared to invest in risky endeavors. Can you make money on bubble investment? Sure. I have family members that doubled their money almost overnight in cryptocurrency and certain stocks. They did not take out a second mortgage to do so!

Think long and hard before taking out that second mortgage. Is it possible to hold off on the renovations or remodeling until you can pay cash? Would it make sense to work one more year before going back to school? What happens to your home if you have a decrease in income and can't make the payments on the second mortgage? The same thing applies to home improvement loans. A second mortgage should always be your last choice except for unusual or desperate situations.

Medical Debt

Medical debt can get out of hand quickly. Many insurance policies require you to pay thousands of dollars each year before insurance kicks in. Try to get a policy with a low deductible so that you aren't stuck with thousands of dollars of debt. If you have many medical bills (I have seen people with over 30 different medical bills totaling thousands of dollars) and medical debt comprises most of your debt, use these priorities:

1. Pay off brand new bills as fast as possible
2. Pay off medical bills sent to collection agencies
3. Pay off older bills starting with the lowest amounts.
4. Pay off the older bills and work your way to the newest.
5. If you owe large amounts from more than five years and have not heard anything from the hospital or doctor, find out if the debt was written off. If not, make it the last debt you pay.

Fund Allocation Recommendations

There are many strategies available in books and websites that suggest percentages and priorities for eliminating debt. I have seen strategies that involved paying off all high interest loans and credit cards first. Other strategies involve either paying the smallest creditor first and working up to the largest or paying each of your creditors a percentage each payday. Debt consolidation companies want you to consolidate all of your debts into one large loan. The book "Richest Man in Babylon" by George S. Clason recommends the following ratios for apportioning your income:

10%	Savings and investments
70%	Living expenses
20%	Debt reduction

I would like to modify these recommendations. First, I will expand on the Living Expenses. If you recall the budget example in Chapter Three, Bob and Sally were trying to free up 20% of their income for savings and debt reduction. 10% of their living expenses was designated for tithing. If you are starting from scratch and have been spending 100% of your income, it may take some time to reach 10% Savings, 20% Debt reduction and 10% Tithing (or Charity giving). I am going to assume that if you are not already giving 10% of your income, you will be working to reach that goal as quickly as possible. Whether or not you do so is between you and your conscience.

With this in mind, let's look at some scenarios based on how much money you can free up because you have eliminated wasteful, unnecessary and unplanned spending. Each scenario will assume that you were initially spending close to 100% of your income and were not giving. They will also assume that you are already paying minimum payments on your various credit accounts like mortgage, credit cards, etc. Only the amount paid above minimum payments will be considered as debt reduction.

10% Freed Up

5%	Giving
5%	Savings
90%	Living Expenses

20% Freed Up

10%	Giving
10%	Savings
80%	Living Expenses

25% Freed Up

10%	Giving
10%	Savings
5%	Debt Reduction
75%	Living Expenses

30% Freed Up

10%	Giving
10%	Savings
10%	Asset Building
70%	Living Expenses

40% Freed Up

10%	Giving
10%	Savings
10%	Debt Reduction
10%	Asset Building
60%	Living Expenses

Some of my readers are trying to build assets, whether through starting their own business or investing. You may have noticed that I didn't list Asset Development until 30% of income has been freed up. You may recall that the budget examples had 10% Tithing built into them. Bob and Sally freed up 30% of their income, not 20%. Your mentor may suggest other percentages to disburse the money you have freed up than I have listed. Listen to your mentor. These numbers are only a guide.

If you have 3-6 months of expenses set aside and you are relatively debt-free, then you would be able to use the following percentages:

20% Freed Up with Savings in Place and No Debt

10%	Giving
10%	Asset Development
80%	Living Expenses

If you have significant debt and have not built up your savings to at least $1000, you should hold off on starting a business or investing in anything until you have gained control of your spending and have freed up at least 30% of your income. This may seem extreme, but how seriously do you want to leave mediocrity and achieve financial security? If you are serious, then you will ruthlessly trim the fat off your spending and apply self-discipline to your finances.

As a rule of thumb, you should devote 10% of your income towards debt reduction and 10% towards savings until you have built up your savings to equal at least three months of expenses. Once you have the savings in place you should raise your percentage of debt reduction to 20% of your income.

Add up all your consumer debt. If your consumer debt exceeds 20% of your annual income, then you will need to adjust your debt reduction spending to a higher level. After your savings are in place, your focus needs to be on reducing your debt to a manageable level. Let's suppose you are bringing home $100,000 net income and you have $40,000 of consumer debt. Your debt is equal to 40% of your annual income. If you devote 10% of your income to debt reduction it will take at least four years to eliminate your consumer debt.

Prioritizing Debt Payments

So, you have gotten your Head out of The Sand and have started allocating money toward debt reduction. Now you are probably wondering how to spread out this money among your creditors? Every person's situation is different with a unique combination of income, debt, obligations and willingness to make things better. All I can do is give some general recommendations unless I am sitting down with you in person. This is the role of a mentor.

After you have listed your income, recurring expenses, bills and debts, you need to sit down with someone who can look at your unique situation and give personalized recommendations. Unless you are dealing with major amounts of debt (more than a year of income) and multiple types of debt, don't waste the money on an accountant. If all the debt you are dealing with totals less than $200,000 you should be able to do the math and make decisions with a mentor. If you are dealing with a complex situation involving large sums of money, especially one that involves business and/or IRS debt, then get an accountant or lawyer to help you.

Passive vs Active Debt

Passive debt is debt that is just sitting there. Some passive debt requires occasional communication with the creditor to keep it passive. Other passive debt includes debt that has been written off by the creditor or handed off to a collection agency that has stopped collection activity. Medical debt more than two years old often falls into this category. Passive debt also includes debt that

110

you are already making minimum payments for and for which you receive monthly statements, not demands for payment.

Active debt is debt that you are receiving collection activity about. If you are receiving demands for payment or phone calls about a debt, it is active. Active debt usually has a negative effect on your credit score and can result in advance collection activity such as litigation, foreclosure, repossession, garnishment of your paycheck and having your bank accounts frozen. Don't let this happen to you. Contact every creditor on your list that is active and explain the situation. Ask if they are willing to work with you and try to make a payment arrangement that allows you to pay other debts. If you are making regular payments, a judge will normally find in your favor, even if the payments are small.

I have heard and read suggestions that you should pay off the high interest debt first and then work on other debt. I understand the reasoning and even agree to an extent. You need to rid yourself of any debt involving title loans, payday loans, pawn shops and other dubious check cashing loan shop loans as fast as you can. But first you must turn your active debt into passive debt. This can often be accomplished, at least temporarily, with a phone call and a token payment.

While you are building your savings cushion, you need to buy yourself some time by aggressively changing all your active debt to passive debt. Make sure to keep your word. If you promise to make a $10 payment to a creditor, make the payment.

Proposed Debt Payment Priorities

The following list is my suggestion for how to prioritize the payment of your debts. Your situation might require different priorities.

1. Address any debt in danger of advanced collection activity
2. Change active debt to passive debt
3. Pay off active debt that stays active
4. Reduce the number of debts by paying off as many small debts as possible.
5. Pay off high interest loans
6. Pay off or pay down credit cards
7. Pay off passive debt
8. Pay off car loans
9. Pay off education loans
10. Pay off mortgage

Don't Miss Out on Opportunity Because You Didn't Get Your Head Out of The Sand

Suppose you have been approached about joining a team of business owners associated with any of the many legitimate Network Marketing companies. You are told that you would need to free up around 10% of your income to have the best chance for success in the opportunity. Please understand that the 10% necessary for successfully building an asset should be AFTER Tithing, Savings and Debt Reduction are accounted for. No one can promise you success if you try to start any business without first gaining control of your finances. It won't be the investment's fault. It won't be the Network Marketing Company's fault. It won't be the fault of the person who introduced you to the opportunity. It will be your fault that you don't succeed, because you did not take control of your finances and did not have the financial self-discipline necessary be successful in any opportunity. Taking on new debt or new financial commitments when you haven't lightened your load is irresponsible. If the opportunity is good enough, it will either still be there when you get your act together, or another opportunity will come along later. Ask the person who is offering the opportunity if they will be willing to mentor you concerning your finances or point you to someone who can.

Occasionally, someone who is suffering from major financial storms can overcome their situation and succeed in an endeavor that would cause failure in the average person. If you accept mentorship and work diligently at controlling your finances and apply yourself mightily to the endeavor, you can succeed. I have met people that have overcome incredible odds. But let me ask you something. If you knew that applying yourself diligently for several months to straightening out your finances would make it much easier to succeed, would it make sense to concentrate on the finances first? If you are looking at a good opportunity and were given this book, grab the opportunity with both hands and get your finances squared away as quickly as possible.

If you are the person offering someone an opportunity, understand that if that person doesn't gain control over their finances, they will probably fail, and you will have wasted your time and your money. You are doing them and yourself no favors if you "sign someone up" who has no resources, no savings, high debt, no control over their finances and no desire to change them. If they want to succeed and they ask you to mentor them, you should guide them in setting up a realistic budget and debt reduction plan. Hold them accountable. If they show themselves to be serious about changing their financial situation, then they will take the opportunity seriously. If they won't be accountable in their finances, then you should seriously consider withdrawing your offer of partnership and mentorship. The inability to be accountable with finances is a huge red flag that needs to be resolved before you make the mistake of partnering with someone.

Please understand that I am not saying that a person must be debt-free with thousands of dollars in the bank before they can invest or build an asset. However, a person who is unable or unwilling to discipline their own spending and has an out-of-control financial situation is not normally a good candidate for partnership in an asset producing business. On the other hand, someone who accepts coaching and mentorship and makes the necessary moves to bring their finances under control is worth devoting time to. It may take someone who is seriously attempting to bring their finances under control a year before they are able to dedicate 10% of their income into a business opportunity. That year can be used for mentorship, personal development, character building and financial stabilization.

Action Steps

1. Write down the amount of money you have freed up or plan to free up by trimming your expenses.

   _____

2. Decide what percentage of income and how many dollars are you can allocate towards the following categories over the next year:

   Savings   _____% $_____

   Debt Reduction   _____% $_____

   Asset Building   _____% $_____

3. List three nagging debts that are currently active and check them off when you have turned them into passive debt.

   a._____

   b._____

   c. _____

   d._____

GET YOUR HEAD OUT OF THE SAND

Chapter 7
Financial Tools and Software

Why You Need to Use Finance Software

Before the days of Debit Cards, people had three main choices when they wanted to purchase something. They could use a check, cash or money order. Every box of checks came with a register. People who were responsible with their finances would diligently enter every transaction onto their register. They always knew exactly what their balance was. They would not write a check unless there was money in the bank to cover it. In contrast, there were people who lived on the edge and would write checks they couldn't cover in the hopes that their payday would arrive before the check hit their bank. Even though they were constantly taking chances, most of them knew their bank balance and exactly how long it took for a check to clear. The penalty for bouncing a check was often extreme, but usually did not result in prosecution unless you failed to pay what you owed. I can remember playing that game early in our marriage. I remember being stressed out hoping the check would clear.

As Debit and eventually Visa Check cards became the norm, it became almost impossible to use a check register to account for everything. With the advent of online banking, online bill payments and a society that routinely used multiple credit cards, it became even harder. One other factor that makes paper accounting extremely difficult is that most couples have two cards for each account. Unless they both diligently record their transactions daily, the paper check register will become a total mess. If you are not using finance software and have no plans to do so, then I would strongly suggest using the envelope system for daily expenses and only use the cards for online purchases and bill payments. If you do not use the envelope system, you must use finance software if you want to have any hope of tracking your money.

An early solution to the complexities of electronic payments was the now defunct Microsoft Money. Microsoft Money and most of the Finance Software that followed are, at their core, electronic check registers. When Microsoft Money first came out, you had to manually enter all your transactions from printouts. Eventually it became possible to download a file containing the transactions and then more recently the software would connect directly to the bank and automatically update all the accounts.

Unfortunately, millions of consumers who did not use finance software had no idea what their bank balance was and would find themselves inundated with NSF (Non-Sufficient Funds) fees. Banks introduced overdraft protection, but NSF charges are still a major source of income for most Banks and Credit Unions. There are only two ways to avoid being blindsided by multiple NSF Charges. The first, which should be everyone's goal, is to keep enough money in the bank so that you always have a minimum balance of around $500. In fact, many banks will charge a fee if your balance goes below $500.

The second way to avoid NSF fees is to track all your expenses and know exactly what is scheduled to be withdrawn from your accounts. It is not enough to check your balance. Your bank doesn't know if you wrote a check. Your balance doesn't include bills that have been set up for automatic payment. You need to have an electronic equivalent of a paper check register that allows entries for future transactions. I started with Microsoft Money and then switched over to Intuit Quicken when Microsoft Money was no longer available. I can look back at ten years of finances numbering over 15,000 transactions. If you track your finances through finance software, and keep aware of your balances, there is no reason you should ever overdraft an account again.

I download the transactions from the bank every day and identify and classify each transaction. This takes a time investment of about five minutes each day. The payoff to this investment is huge. I always know the true state of my finances and am never caught off guard by unexpected expenses. A paper check register will only work if you limit yourself to writing checks or withdrawing cash. It is extremely difficult to use a paper check register to account for electronic transactions. You will only know the true state of your finances if you use software or pay an accountant to use his.

Finance software is not yet perfect. It doesn't know what is going on unless you or the bank tell it. The software doesn't know that you made a credit purchase on your debit card, so if your spouse forgets to mention a purchase, you might be in for a surprise when it clears. Both you and your spouse or partner need to communicate and be onboard with accountability. You need to enter any credit purchase before it shows up online. You must be careful when using a debit card. Sometimes the purchase will go through as credit and will be put on hold for several days. The only way to account for it is to manually enter the transaction and then match it to the downloaded transaction several days later.

When worked properly, finance software will show you exactly what your current financial condition is. It will also accurately forecast the future, if (and this is a big IF) you stay true to your spending plan. Finance software reduces the time necessary to track your money, assets, liabilities, income and investments. It also makes it easier to file your taxes, especially if you take the time to categorize your income and expenses. The initial setup will take time and effort. I would recommend downloading all your transactions for the past 12 months when you get started.

Types of Finance Software
Spreadsheets

Spreadsheets are wonderful tools that can be customized to match almost any situation. They can be set up to automatically do the math, which is a time saver. There is a learning curve necessary to get full use out of them and they must be kept up to date to be useful.

To use spreadsheets, you must have spreadsheet software. The most widely used spreadsheet software is Microsoft Excel, which comes with Microsoft Office. If you don't have access to Microsoft Office, there are several free options available. The two most common free office suites available are Libre Office and Open Office. Either one will work for you. I strongly recommend using a spreadsheet to set up a basic budget that deals with general categories. This will set up the framework necessary to successfully manage your finances with finance software.

I have seen budget spreadsheets that were works of art. They have beautiful colors, multiple sections and were so complicated that only a professional could use them. Other budget spreadsheets are simpler but require manipulation of the spreadsheet to match anything other than the most general financial situation. Unfortunately, while the average person can use a prepared spreadsheet, most people have little experience in manipulating one. If you know how to build a spreadsheet, then it is easy to build one that will fit your circumstances. If not, then you will need to use a spreadsheet that someone else has prepared.

I have found that the best use of spreadsheets in budgeting is for listing income, debts and recurring expenses. A spreadsheet is also good for creating a basic budget, especially when some of the categories are based on percentages of income and debt. Spreadsheets are good tools for performing calculations dealing with income and expenses. Spreadsheets help develop a general picture of your financial situation but are

121

generally not flexible enough to be used for future planning without becoming so complex that they are difficult to use and keep up with. If your mentor doesn't have a basic budget spreadsheet available, you can download one from my website www.gyhootsbook.com

Mint

Mint is a web-based financial software that has many benefits, the biggest being that it is free. It can help you set up a budget and it will monitor your accounts. It will help you set and reach financial goals as well as set up a savings plan. If you don't have financial software, this is an excellent way to start. Mint is simple to use and has many features that will make you feel like a professional.

The main drawback of Mint is that it doesn't currently allow for forecasting like Quicken does. However, Mint will keep you current on all your expenses and help you to stay on top of your financial condition. It will download from the banks on a schedule that you set and then notify you if there is a low balance. It also allows you to set up recurring bills, both online and offline.

A feature of Mint that is very useful is the phone app. You can monitor your accounts from your phone. This is very helpful if you want to check on the status of multiple accounts and see how well you are keeping to your budget. It is not my job to endorse any software, but I will say that Mint is sufficient to track normal household budgets. Where Mint runs into problems is if you have multiple incomes from sources such as rental income, annuities, investments and multiple businesses.

Use Mint if your financial situation is relatively simple. If your situation is complicated, you may need to look at other options.

Quicken

Quicken is the software that I use for tracking my personal and business income. There are several versions available. The most expensive and useful version is the Home Business and Rental Income version. If you have income from investments, rental properties, self-employment or home-based business, then Quicken will fulfill your needs. If you are running a business that needs to be separate from your personal finances, then you need Quick Books or an accountant. Quicken also has a basic version that is relatively inexpensive for people with simple budgeting requirements. If you plan on having a job for the rest of your life and don't plan to invest or build assets, then you can use either Quicken Basic or Mint.

One of the most useful features of Quicken is the ability to add pending income, expenses and transfers in the Bills tab. You can set up transactions for one time, yearly, monthly, weekly or almost any frequency you can imagine. Let's say that you know that you have a net paycheck of $2500 every other Friday and your spouse's paycheck is $700 on the 1st and 15th of the month. When you enter these as pending transactions, Quicken automatically accounts for them and allows you to see in chart form what your future balances will be. Of course, no one has income with no expenses unless they are living in their parent's basement. You also need to set up pending expenses for all your recurring expenses and budget items such as rent, mortgage, utilities, groceries, tithing, EZ-Pass, etc. Pending Transfers are extremely useful. I use them to show planned transfers to savings accounts, as well as planned cash withdrawals for the envelope system.

If you are using an envelope system (which we discussed in Chapter Four) Quicken has a feature that is extremely helpful. You can and should set up accounts for every one of your creditors, utilities and anything you have an account with, such as medical bills and credit cards. You should also set up an account called Petty Cash. This is the account for cash withdrawals and payments. If you are using the envelope system, you should set up an account for any envelope that will experience multiple purchases. If you are using spreadsheets or Mint, you need to keep all your receipts in the envelope and enter the transactions each week. Quicken saves you from having multiple receipts in envelopes or the floor of your car by allowing you to take a picture of the receipt and entering the transaction details onto the phone app. The receipt is now attached to the transaction, so if you ever need a copy, it will be available for examination or printing.

Quicken also has the advantage of being able to transfer tax data directly to some tax software. This is helpful when you have taken the time to create the necessary categories and separate personal from business transactions. When done right, you will be able to see at a glance exactly how much you spent for any taxable category.

Other Options

There are other less well known financial software programs available. Your mentor may suggest one that I haven't listed. If so, listen to your mentor. Some examples include Quick Books Self-Employed, and several good finance programs available for people using the Linux Operating System. Banks are starting to provide basic online finance tracking and if all your accounts are in one bank, this may be a good option for you. Whichever option you choose, spend the time to properly set things up. Then invest a few minutes every day to keep yourself current on your financial situation.

Feel free to explore different options for finance software. There are too many products out there for this book to cover them all in any detail. Make sure to check user reviews and security reports, especially for web-based software. Act today. If you are not able to buy software now, then use a free web-based program like Mint. Don't wait. Do it now. You won't regret it.

GET YOUR HEAD OUT OF THE SAND

Afterword

I hope that this book has provided the breakthrough that you needed to gain control of your finances. If all you do is Identify, Classify, Justify and Modify your expenses, you will greatly improve your situation. If you take the next steps and build a realistic budget based on actual history instead of guesswork and then keep totally aware of every dollar that passes through your keeping, you will have gotten your head out of the sand and become the master of your money instead of your money's servant.

It isn't enough to read this book. You need to act. Find a mentor. Keep yourself accountable. Check your balances and transactions daily. Modify your recurring expense sheet and budget as circumstances change. Review your goals and speak them.

Read the following paragraph out loud:

I am the master of my finances. Every dollar that comes my way is assigned a purpose. I practice delayed gratification and self-control always. I am in control of my money. I give at least ten percent of my income to good causes and do not even miss it. I always consult with someone before making a major purchase. I pay cash or cash equivalent for all purchases.

Copy these statements onto a notecard or write your own present tense statements of how you control your finances. Repeat them every day and memorize them. Be prepared for results beyond what you ever thought possible.

Lawrence J. Mast served in the United States Army for eleven years in the Reserves as a Pharmacy Technician and eight years on active duty as a Watercraft Operator at Fort Eustis, VA. He graduated from Old Dominion University with a bachelor's degree in English Professional Writing in 2014.

He likes to fish, work out at the gym, watch trains, play guitar and write songs. He can often be found at ponds feeding the turtles or at the Amtrak station doing train and people watching. He is an avid reader and averages a book every two days. His favorite hobby is storm chasing and he has managed to film several tornados in Virginia, Tennessee and Missouri.

Larry met Patty Christiana at Fort Sam Houston in San Antonio, TX and asked her to marry him three weeks later. They have been married for 33 years and have three sons, two daughters and three grandchildren. Both his daughters and one son have served or are currently serving in the US military.

"DREAM BIG. THINK BIG. SPEND SMALL."

58378223R00076

Made in the USA
Columbia, SC
24 May 2019